Black and White Love

Agata Walker

*to
Mrs Bowen

from
Agata Walker
Adam Sniady's
mother.*

Published by New Generation Publishing in 2021

Copyright © Agata Walker 2021

First Edition

The author asserts the moral right under the Copyright, Designs and Patents Act 1988 to be identified as the author of this work.

All Rights reserved. No part of this publication may be reproduced, stored in a retrieval system or transmitted, in any form or by any means without the prior consent of the author, nor be otherwise circulated in any form of binding or cover other than that which it is published and without a similar condition being imposed on the subsequent purchaser.

ISBN   978-1-80369-170-1

www.newgeneration-publishing.com

 New Generation Publishing

About the Author

Agata Walker was born in Poland. She has qualifications of pharmacy technician gained in Medical College in Szczecin. She has 3 children. The oldest one Melania is making vlogs on YouTube. She has been doing that many years. Her YouTube channel is called Melania Vlogs. Agata's son is in the last year of Sixth Form and wants to become accountant one day. The little one is in Year1 of primary school. She loves to go to her school. Agata's husband is still supporting although he had been through a lot falling in love with a white woman'.

Thank you to Patricia, Jonas, my mother, my father, auntie Jola, Phill and Margaret for enabling me to come to Great Britain.

CHAPTER 1

We were on our way to Jamaica with children when I was in UK for the first time. We were just passing through changing airports from Heathrow to Gatwick by National Express bus. I was even stopped at Heathrow airport by Immigration for a few minutes while they were checking something. Fortunately they let us through the boarder. It happened in times when Poland wasn't a part of EU yet.

I'm Polish but my husband is Jamaican. We met in Switzerland for the first time and the rest is history.

I liked the country. All these houses are made of red bricks. Motorways and countryside.

I needed a lot of assistance on the airports because I was travelling with 2 little children, pram and luggage. Pawel was only a few months old only and Ewa one and a half. So it was quite difficult journey to make.

But I had to make it. I was going to marry John. Our plan was to get married and move to England to live. Why England? They were many Jamaicans and Polish people in this country. Besides we tried to make it in my country but we didn't succeed. John ended up being illegal in Poland and he was sent back home by Police. He couldn't come back to Poland for 5 years. Immigration law is tough. We didn't manage to get married on time. John's visa was expired and that was it. They didn't care that we had a child and I was pregnant again at that time. No chance for us. John didn't do nothing wrong but was held in deportation center for a few weeks in Szczecin. That's the way it is. Without proper papers nothing can be done in a strange country.

Our life with John wasn't easy from the beginning. My family in Poland persecuted us because I fell in love with a black man, which was hard for us to experience. I quickly became pregnant and that didn't help the situation. It made it worse.

When I was growing up I lived like in a bubble. My family had never had problems with money. Father worked abroad and mother wasn't working. I didn't even know back then that people needed money to survive in this world. That's how lucky I was.

I was 24 when we met with John. I had just finished my Medical College. I even had managed to get a job in Szczecin before our meeting with John, which I canceled afterwards. Maybe it was a mistake. I would be financially independent with my own career. But I simply didn't have an idea how money and work were important. That's the lesson I was going to learn pretty soon. Love only cannot put food on our tables and roof over our heads. Love cannot pay our bills.

World is created in certain way and we have to accept it. My attitude towards life was 'God will provide'. But in reality is 'God provides those who provide themselves.

I am happy now, but there were times when it was tough. Especially after Ewa and Pawel were born and I was alone with them in Poland. I had no help whatsoever. The same in London when we were alone waiting for John to join us for a few months. We were homeless for a day, sometimes hungry, begging for money. I will never forget these days. Now I know everybody can go down in life like me. We all should appreciate what we've got and not to take it for granted.

John grew up in Jamaica raised by his grandparents in countryside. Jamaica is a third world country. His childhood was different than mine, but still he was happy as a child. They weren't rich but it wasn't important to them. They had this special bond and he always remembered that. Nothing after his childhood and young years until his thirties will never be the same again. He loved his life in Jamaica. That's why it was so hard to adjust to British reality at first. Up to this day, after 10 years in England, he still calls Jamaica his home and misses it, which make me mad sometimes. Like he doesn't appreciate what we have here and cannot be happy.

John is complaining a lot about me and kids, which is quite hurtful to me to hear. He doesn't feel proud of Ewa, Pawel and Emilia although Ewa is sick, Pawel is doing well at school and Emilia is such a sweetheart.

When Ewa was about 12 years old she turned against John one time. We didn't know back then that she was sick. She kicked John and he fell on the table. He was just trying to touch her playfully, while coming back from work. When Ewa was 14 years old she was diagnosed with autism. She spent 3 months in a hospital Priory in Birmingham. It was difficult time for our family. Since then she has been on medication and doing quite well, but we always have to be careful with her. She sometimes is not stable and cannot be trusted.

I am the one who fully understand her because I am on the same medication as she. I don't have autism. I suffer from bipolar disorder. I was diagnosed with it in 2008. But it wasn't the first time me having problems with my mental health. First psychotic episode I experienced being just 19 years old. So it runs in the family. Fortunately Pawel is healthy and Emilia too.

John, as I said before, is also complaining about me. I don't work now and I haven't been working for almost 3 years now.

John wishes we were a team, but he doesn't feel we are because I don't contribute anything financially to our family budget.

I don't know what is my problem with working. I just know I don't like to be far from home and alone. My occupation is pharmacy technician with qualifications gained in Poland. I have some issues with people generally. Like I am scared of them, I mean strangers. I think nobody is like me.

Besides the last 3 years were especially hard for me. I was experiencing during these years side effects of my medicine. While I was working in hospital in Birmingham approximately once a week I had to come back home a few hours earlier because I couldn't bring my eyes down. I wasn't able to continue my shift because I couldn't control my eyes. I didn't see anything on the computer and things like that. People around me in this pharmacy could see that something was wrong with me. After a few months of work like that I was dismissed, which was bad for me. This was my one and only hospital job. I was devastated to lose it.

Thankfully now I don't have these side effects any more and I feel good. I have my medicines changed recently by my psychiatrist. I am so grateful to him for that. He told me on my last appointment in December that I would be able to work again.

In January even I managed to get a job in popcorn factory, but as usual I lasted 3 days there. I don't last long in places like that. Never ever. Jobs like that it's easy to get and easy to lose, which is a shame.

John is also disappointed with our baby Emilia. She is 4 years old. She basically tells the worse things about him, and he blames me for that. He says I'm bringing her up in the wrong way.

I am always telling him that people never change. Situations change, but people stay the same.

Also relationships between people change with time (if you give them time). John doesn't like Ewa any more somehow. It's worrying me, but I'm just waiting when she will be on her own independent one day in the nearest time, so he might start to like her again.

She will be 18 years old next month. She used to want to become hair dresser in secondary school. Now she is doing Media in her college and she likes it. First year they were doing a lot of photography. This year filming. She enjoys making vlogs. That is her hobby.

Next year she will be studying Performing Arts. She wants to become an actress now. Ewa is arty like me. But John doesn't treat her seriously. He basically says she is wasting time in college. He wishes she would become a police woman or an army worker.I sometimes have a feeling that I don't believe in her too much although I should. Who should believe in her if not me? She is quite self-confident, which is good for her.

Unlike Pawel. Pawel is shy. John would like Pawel to be like him, who 'doesn't give a fuck about anybody', but he isn't.

A few years ago my son was in a football team. Every Sunday we were taking him to the pitches, which were situated mostly in the parks, so he could play matches. Pawel was so happy. I was so proud of him. I am not big fan of football, but my son is, so I was happy for him every Sunday. But John was only criticizing him. Most of the time he was playing in defense. He had never scored a goal. My husband had never told him his criticism in the face. He was always telling me. Whatever I do or my children John always fills me with the doubts. I shouldn't let him do that. My believes are my believes. I have to protect them. Without this attitude I will never succeed in life. Never ever. Now when I am in my forties I am sure of that.

John used to have many relationship with women before me. He has altogether 5 children with 3 different Jamaican women. So he can compere us. But I am not Jamaican and I will never be one. I am not better or worse, but I'm different. John often says that nobody in this world is like me. I don't know why he says that. I take it as a compliment always.

The true about me is that in my childhood I wasn't taught by my mother to do anything. She didn't work. The whole time she was a housewife taking care of me and my 5 years younger brother, and the house, while my father was at work as a sea man most of the time somewhere abroad. Mother was with us with Thomas (that's my brother's name) from the morning till evening. That's how fortunately we were.

The reason why my mother didn't teach me anything was that she didn't want to be disturb. She preferred to do everything herself without anybody's help. That's the way she has always been and she is still like that now. When we come with children to visit my parents in Poland (we try to do that every summer) she even doesn't let me wash the dishes.

But to be honest I still cannot cook Polish food. I hadn't learnt myself since then. although everybody in my family likes this food except from Emilia. She has already been to Poland 2 times. She cannot speak Polish language. My youngest daughter was born in UK. Ewa and Pawel were born in Poland and even managed to learn Polish language in reading, speaking and writing, because they both attended first 2 years (Pawel 1) primary school in Poland, so they are bilingual. Emilia cannot talk to grandparents, so they couldn't really get to know her yet. She likes them, She misses them. Emilia likes Poland a lot, but they cannot communicate, because of language barrier. The same problem has John.

It's difficult to translate from one language to another when you are personally involved with people you are translating for. How can I translate between my mother and my husband when they have conversation about me for example? Good things about myself I can translate, but bad I would rather pretend they are not said. Or translating conversation about something I am not interested in, for example cooking. It's boring to talk about, so what about translating it?

In John's opinion being bilingual is bad. That's why before Emilia was born he had asked me to talk to her in English only. It's very hard for me, although it has been over 4 years now since my baby girl was born. It's hard because my first language is Polish and it will always will be. It's natural to use it talk to my children. To talk to them in English it always feels fake, and it will always be like that, I think so. When I speak in my language I it's easy. I'm relax and I enjoyed it. I can speak English very well, but most of times I think in Polish, so I have to constantly translate in my head, which is like a double job.

Besides there is another big issue when you live with people who speak different languages. I mean when your family is mixed from various countries like mine. Ewa and Pawel are Polish speakers. Ewa also can write and read in Polish. She even passed GCSEs in that language. We write text messages in Polish.

Pawel speaks also Polish, but when I am the one to talk to him I always have to ask him to repeat it once, sometimes even twice. That's annoying. Like I am deaf, or he cannot speak properly any more. I just don't like to make him feel uncomfortable. I don't know about him, but it definitely makes me feel uncomfortable.

The biggest problem in my household is between me and John. He doesn't understand most of things we talk about with my two eldest children, and sometimes he gets angry. I think it's because he thinks somebody from us is talking bad things about him.

He also doesn't like when I talk to my parents on the phone. They are my parents and I will always talk to them, especially that we don't see one another very often. They had already come to visit us three times since we are in England. I used to visit them every summer with children. Since Emilia was born we were going every two years. The first year she didn't have a passport. When she was three we couldn't go because I was working in a hospital and couldn't get holidays. This year Ewa went to visit grandparents. She had just turned sixteen that year. She went by plane from Liverpool to Szczecin. Grandparents collected her from the airport. She spent three weeks there.

My mother would like us to come every summer Swinoujscie, where they live, is situated on the coast of Baltic Sea. She thinks that we go to visit her only because there is nice beach. But when we go we don't care about beach too much. We just go to spend some time with my mother and father. And also I help my mother in her shop. It is a shop with medicines and herbs.

We were there last summer. Even John came to visit for a few days. Usually we spend at their place around 6 weeks with children. We all like Poland. But the more years pass since we live abroad, the more distant I feel from Polish reality.

At the beginning I missed everything so much from my country. Especially my parents, but also places I used to like, and I was familiar with. I didn't have a lot of friends, and I hardly ever saw my younger brother. So that's it. Nothing else to miss. My children were, and are always with me. They are the most important in my life.

I remember I was lying in my bed during those first months in Britain, trying to fall asleep, but I couldn't. I saw those places in my mind, over and over again. Things like flowers in Szczecin on the estate, where we used to live with children. The place was called Osiedle Bukowe, and I liked it there very much back in the days. Or my way to work, which I made every day from Monday to Friday. It was so close to our flat to get to that work. Fifteen minutes down the hill. Or our shopping with Ewa in Szczecin in those big supermarkets

To remember is a good thing, but not always. Sometimes it's good to forget. Especially when you were forced to leave your beautiful country, because of beautiful and good people, who suddenly became ugly and not good any more.

CHAPTER 2

After our wedding in Jamaica I had to find my way to United Kingdom. I wanted us with children to be reunited with John as soon as possible. It wasn't so difficult to do that.

Margaret is John's sister, who lives in Switzerland. John used to live in her house when we first met. We went to visit her with children a few years months after the wedding, and spent with her a few weeks in the summer.

She is a hard-working woman. Her husband is Swiss, and they bring up 3 children together.

Switzerland is a beautiful place. People are so relax there, not in a rush. Everybody knows what to do.

Unlike me. I didn't know what I was doing, coming to visit Margaret and her family with two small children without any money, with their father in distant Jamaica. It was hard.

Margaret is a little older than me. She used to be in UK for some time, working a long time ago. She lived than in her cousins' house, whose name is Patricia.

We had a good time with Ewa and Pawel in Lausanne with Margaret, and her family. She is good at entertaining people. Margaret loves to throw parties, going clubbing and travelling all over the world. She even took us for a trip to Italy by car to Genova for one night. It's a beautiful town. We visited an Aquarium there.

At the end of our stay there was birthday party of her youngest son. It was a garden party.

We came back home just after this party to Poland.

After we had come back from Switzerland, I got a call from Margaret. She said that her cousin Patricia invited me to her place.

I was so happy, and grateful to Margaret. She gave me Patricia's address over the phone.

It was time to make a plan for me. I had to arrange childcare, because I wanted to go to England all by myself.

I wrote a letter to my favorite auntie. She was my mother's sister (sadly she is not with us any more, she passed away seven years ago). Her name was Mariola, but everybody called her Jola.

Auntie Jola used to live far from we were lived. It's about seven hundred kilometers distance. But sometimes she was always close to us when I was a child. We spent a lot of time together, and I liked her very much. She even christened me in church, when I was about six years old. My parents weren't there at my christening. Auntie Jola was my Godmother.

We had a lot of fun together. She took me everywhere with her. Shopping, walks, to her favorite club to play games and even to the swimming-pool, which I liked the most. At home we were playing cards together, baking cakes. We were painting our nails, doing our hair, and things like that. Auntie Jola was like a idol to me, and I always looked out to her.

In that letter I asked her to come to Swinoujscie to help my parents to look after my children.

Of course she didn't let me down. She came as soon as she could, and I was able to go to England on my own. Ewa was two years old, and Pawel was so small, that he couldn't even walk yet. I had never left them before like that. But this time I had to.

A few days later, after my auntie had come, I was on my mission. I took a bus from Szczecin to Birmingham, and left my babies behind me for a few days. But it felt like I was doing the right thing. I just wanted my family to be completed again, my children to have father, and me my husband back.

I had never been in UK before.

Birmingham seemed to be very modern city, which I liked very much.

When I reached there, I was exhausted after twenty four hours journey. My bus left me at the Coach Station in Digbeth in the City Center.

I had Patricia's address and telephone number. I kept asking everybody how to get there by bus, but nobody knew the place.

Finally, someone from those strangers, who I met, being lost in Birmingham, helped me a lot. I think it was a one man in a wheelchair. He had called Patricia from his mobile, and luckily, she picked it up. It occurred that the address I had was different than the one Margaret had given me. It was going to be Pelsall, not Telsall

Thanks to this phone call, this man on the bus, Patricia knew I was coming. She came out to meet me on the bus stop. She greeted me, and help me with my luggage.

Her house wasn't far from the bus stop at all. She let me in, and introduced me to her husband Phill. We talked a little bit, drinking a cup of tea, and eating biscuits. Afterwards she showed me my room, which was upstairs. These people seemed to be friendly, and I felt well in their house.

But I didn't go there only to visit them, or sightseeing. I came there with one intention to get information how to invite John to the UK as a EU citizen.

Patricia sent me to this wonderful place called Citizen's Advice Bureau (CAB). They helped me a lot this first time. I didn't even know back then how many more times they were going to help me in the future. Very many.

I was waiting quite a long time, before I was seen by an adviser. I got information that I needed, and useful form. I was so happy. Time to meet my love again was coming closer, and closer.

I had to have a job in England and be registered with Home Office. To invite John I had to post to him this certificate of registration, and a few more documents. He had to apply for visa in Embassy in Kingston, Jamaican capital.

Later on I spent a few more days with Patricia and Phill. She occurred to be such a positive, and energetic character. Phill was rather serious, but easy to talk to.

At that time they were dreaming about having a child together. Patricia have two sons from previous marriage. They were sixteen and nineteen years old.

Regrettably now we live with my family quite close to Patricia's house, but we don't see each other often. Particularly me. I don't even remember, when did I last see her.

A few years ago things were different, because now, I'm afraid, Patricia suffers from Alzheimer's disease.

John see them from time to time, and her condition is getting worse.

At the end of my stay in Pelsall, I was left alone by Patricia and Phill. They were going to visit Jamaica, and left me alone for two or three days. I was supposed to drop their keys in a letter box in the door, before I was leaving.

These last days in Pelsall were hard for me. I spent all my money, and didn't have money even for food. Shame on me.

But somehow I managed to survive. I think I sold my mobile for money, to buy for myself something to eat. I am not good with money, and I have never been (and most likely I will never be). The problem is that I love shopping. This is my favorite activity. I'm afraid my two daughters are the same.

I had a chance to get to know Patricia's two sons, whose names are Paul and Nathanio. Paul is older than Nathanio. He was a taxi driver. Nathanio was working in Carphone Warehouse.

I spent a few hours with Paul, because he was taking Patricia and Phill to the airport in Manchester, when they were going to Jamaica, and I went with them. We had left them, and we came back to Pelsall together with Paul.

He really impressed me, by the way he was. I was somehow attracted to him, although he was younger than me, and I was married with two little children. He had a girlfriend, and converted into muslim for her.

We were talking a lot during our way back from Manchester about Christianity and Islam.

I was quite happy, when he finally left me alone in Paricia's house because definitely I liked Paul too much. I think he liked me too.

I am a one-man woman. I've never cheated on anybody.

My first boyfriend from High School went for an American dream. After studying one year in Chicago, he never came back to Poland. We were writing letters that first year, but after that I called it a day.

My second boyfriend left me, because I got sick. He was much older than me. It was too much for him to bear.

I never made love with them.

With John it was different. We made love on the second day after we met. He proposed to me on the third day. So we never dated. He was never my boyfriend. We quickly had two children together.

I could never cheat on him with anybody. Even with such a nice man like Paul.

It's natural. Everybody wants to be happy, but sometimes you have to wait. Good things come for those who wait. Like real love.

That's why generally I avoid men as much as I can. Not to put myself in trouble. John is jealous, and I am jealous too. I even like when he is jealous. It's flattering me. It means that he cares.

I can also keep thinking a few days about some girl, he had mentioned to me. For example one time John told me about one Eastern European girl, who worked on Industrial Estate, where was his workplace. All men were watching her passing, because she was so pretty. They called her Queen of an Estate. To make the matters worse she took the same bus as John.

In my imagination I was seeing John on the bus admiring Queen of an Estate, and at the same time forgetting about me. That's just horrible. That's what people do, who have too much free time like me then.

Of course Paul had asked me before he left if I needed any assistance. I quickly said'no'.

On the day of my departure from Pelsall I did, what I had been told to do. I mean to drop the key through the letter box in Patricia's house. I was coming back home to Swinoujscie to my babies.

I took a bus from Birmingham to Szczecin. Because I hadn't asked my father to collect me from Szczecin Bus Station, I had to go by train to Swinoujscie, which made me mad with father again.

It was good to see my children again. I spent in England around ten days. But it's not my style to leave them behind like that.

I thanked my parents and auntie Jola to enable me to leave kids with them, so I could go to UK alone. Auntie came back home, and we were with Ewa and Pawel there, in my parents' house, which John calls white house'.

I exactly knew what to do to move my family to the United Kingdom, and my parents were going to help me, whenever they wanted or not.

CHAPTER 3

It was good to be reunited with the kids, but as usual father was on my case. I had to find a job in UK

There are a lot of agencies in Poland, which were sending Polish people to work abroad. Even my father for many years was working through agencies like that abroad as a sea man.

I was looking for work in healthcare. I'm a pharmacy technician, so I know a lot about medicines, and how to sell them, make them, and about customer service.

After a few weeks of searching some suitable jobs for myself through magazines' adverts I managed to find one as a care assistant in one Care Home in Cornwall. Father of course helped me all the way through, including taking me with children to Gdansk for an interview.

I was successful. I got a job. I signed the contract.

I was over the moon. I had thought before that it wouldn't be so easy.

I finished my Medical College in Szczecin in 2001. Three years before my mother had started to run her herbal shop called 'Melisa'.She had to do the course first to be able to work with medicines and herbs. I did this course just after her in Szczecin University.

So my first job was as a shop assistant in my mother's shop. I didn't know back then what I know now that having your own business, or work for the family is the best work ever. I didn't appreciate it at first. I remember mother paid me 5 zlotych(Polish currency) an hour. Usually I worked there part time.

The shop was doing well, thanks to our efforts.

I was even working there when I was pregnant, and a few weeks after my first daughter was born.

John was with her. I'd had to pump milk for her from my breasts every morning into the bottle before I went to work, because she liked to be breastfed. John was feeding her from this bottle, when I was gone.

After John had been deported from Poland to Jamaica, and I was pregnant with Pawel I knew I had to leave the 'white house' as soon as possible, after all these events.

Quite quickly I found my way out of there. I got a job in hospital in Szczecin. It's a hundred kilometers from Swinoujscie. That's the same place I was going to my Medical College. I like this city.

I was pleased with myself. I had to move out of my parents' house, and move into flat in Szczecin, close to my work place. Of course father found me that flat, and helped me to move in. I don't know how, but my father knew I was pregnant, although I hadn't told anyone about it. To keep a secret I even didn't make an appointment, to check if everything is all right with my baby. I was so ashamed of myself, because of that.

My work in a hospital pharmacy, and life in Szczecin with little Ewa was good. Of course I missed John, but I was sure we would be together again. My parents even didn't know that we were still in touch with him. Every day I sent him a text. Occasionally we talked on the phone, but that was expensive. I was calling from the phone box, using special card.

I was proud of myself. I could make it without parents. I never asked them for money. I was independent, and it felt good.

At the beginning I had some problems with Ewa. She started to go to nursery, but after the first day she didn't feel well. I took her to the doctor, and he sent us to the hospital. She was actually dehydrated, after vomiting, and not drinking at all.

We spent three days in the hospital. Fortunately she got better, and we could leave the hospital.

I decided not to send Ewa to this nursery any more. I quickly found her a nanny. Her name was Lilla, and she came from Ukraine.

I was lucky to find somebody like her. We even became friends.

She took care of Ewa in my flat well.

I was also lucky to find a job like that. There were three pharmacy technicians there (including me), one pharmacist, and two cleaners. I really enjoyed working there.

These two pharmacy technicians seemed to be friendly, but eventually they were going to let me down big time.

I didn't know that these two women were so mad with me, because I was pregnant. We'd never talked about it. But when I finally gave birth to Pawel in the same hospital, where I worked, they even didn't come to visit us. It really hurt my feelings, especially because they knew I was in Szczecin alone. I was waiting for them, but they never came, which was sad.

I thought they were my friends, but I was wrong again.

My work in this hospital lasted a few months. I gave birth to Pawel, and that was it. I never returned there after that event in my life.

When it comes to work I seem to always have an excuse to leave. There is always something more important than working, and earning money. But at all times I'm surprised that I don't have money. Like I don't understand how this world operates.

I am rather serious person. I like to buy kind of things, and I'm mad that I cannot afford something.

The whole my life as an adult I have had, and still have feeling that I'm suffering, because of luck of money. I don't know if it's normal or not.

I wish I could have everything I want to have for myself, and my family.

My husband, for example, is telling me that I'm selfish. He is complaining about that very often. Most of our life together he is working, and having money, not me.

Every year in December, when it's John's birthday, he is unhappy. He blames me for that. Most of the time it's very difficult to please him. Some people from my family, like my mother or my cousin Ewa, told me that John would never be happy. It's just in his blood. I'm doing my best, but it's still not enough. He likes to be alone a lot. I wish we could do more things together. I like to read and write. He likes to watch television. I like to eat sweets. John is a smoker. I walk, while he drives. I don't mind these differences. We still have fun together.

Generally we devoted our lives to children. It's hard to believe, but we've been in the cinema once together. We hardly ever go to restaurants, of pubs. We used to go for walks, but not any more.

I'm not complaining. I'm just saying how things are.

It's because we've never had any help from my family to assist us with childcare, when we lived in Poland, and in England we have no friends. That's why we were, and still are short of quality time as a couple together.

I don't think I want too much from life. I just want all of us to be happy in my family.

I know I am happy.

Especially since Emilia was born. Before I became pregnant, I had been depressed, I guess. Long months, maybe even years, I was at home with not too much to do. I was waking up Ewa and Pawel, and walked them to school. Later on straight to bed. I remember it was hard to get up to make myself some breakfast. I didn't watch television, I didn't read books, I didn't write. Usually, at around two o'clock, I had to get up from my bed to make dinner.

Afternoons were the best for me, because I had kids at home, and in the evening my husband was coming back from work.

I didn't even realize that something was wrong with me.

The only thing that kept me alive in those days was shopping, which we mainly did on Fridays. Of course mostly we only did grocery shopping, but still I enjoyed it the most.

I appreciate everything that we've got. I really do.

In our first house in Pleck (that's also Walsall area) in winter it was always cold. We had almost everywhere were old windows, and no matter how much we charged gas, it wasn't enough to heat up the house. We spend four winters like that in a cold. That was terrible.

Later on John had applied for a council house for us, and when we got it, it was perfect, and still is. Everybody deserves to live like that.

We got three bedroom house with much bigger kitchen, than we had had before, and one big bathroom upstairs, and toilet downstairs. There is even pretty fireplace in the living room.

Pawel chose the smallest bedroom, Ewa big one from the side of the back garden, and we with John took another big bedroom from the side of the street.

It was an exciting time for my family to move the house. We bought some new things to this house, like curtains, carpet, cooker.

First on to move in was John. In the meantime my brother brought my parents, and his wife for a few days to visit us. They came by car.

We like to spend time with grandparents with children. They always buy us something, and take us places. We always have a good time together.

They really liked our new house. My brother and me sister-in –law liked it too.

It's nice to share your happiness with family, and friends, who always wish you well. That's what I miss the most, living in a foreign country, having no friends, far from my family.

A few months after we had had that visit from my family, my brother asked me, if they could come to our place, with his wife Maria, to stay for a few weeks. They were planning to stay in UK for a longer time to find jobs, and place to live.

After conversation with John about it, I said 'yes'.

So soon after this conversation, they came. To be honest, nobody from my family wasn't happy about it. Particularly me, but also children didn't know how to behave. Only John was at ease with their presence.

We put them in the living-room to sleep.

Maria is different than me. She laughs out loud. I'm rather quiet. She is rough with people, while I'm soft and shy.

There is five years gap in age between me and Tom. We were brought up almost separated. He was definitely my mother's favorite.

Maybe five years is not a lot, but Tom and Maria have much more in common with my children, then with me.

They are good with technology like smart phones, and laptops, unlike me. I'm getting better now, but back then I wasn't. When I was in high school in Poland we had DOS as an operating system not WINDOWS yet.

But Ewa and Pawel are so called 'millennium children' are very good with technology. Since Primary School they have been using computers, ipods and laptops. Everything I've learned about these things, I have learnt from them.

Another link between them-X-Box. I couldn't believe that Maria play games like that.

They spend a few weeks in our place. Tom quickly found work in factory in Pleck. Maria also got a job in Tipton in factory, where she was dealing with metal. So they were sorted.

They rented a flat near to our house.

John of course was using their example of success to teach me a lesson. I will never learn.

CHAPTER 4

I got a job with accommodation, but I didn't have any childcare, or money to get there. I was going to go with children to that work in Cornwall. I had never thought it was a bad idea, and that my employer might have problem with that.

My mother volunteered to go with us there, so she could help me to take care of Ewa and Pawel. I was very happy about that. It felt like I was one step closer to our reunion with John. It had been almost halt of a year, since we last saw each other. That's a long time. I was trying not to think about it in that way, to feel sorry for myself, or something like that. But it was hard to be alone. Everything was in my hands. John was just waiting for a sign from me to come. That was a big responsibility.

Father arranged plane tickets for us to London Stanstead Airport in England. I had a lot of luggage. My mother was with us. Nothing could go wrong. Great Britain is closer to Jamaica than Poland. There was only Atlantic Ocean between me and John. Soon he was going to cross it, to be with me and children.

My mother had never been in UK before, and also she had never travelled by plane. So all this experienced was new, and exciting to her.

I was responsible for all of us. My mother couldn't speak English.

We had to wait quite a long time for National Express bus to Plymouth. Perranporth, the place where I was going to work, is close to Plymouth.

It was a few hours on the bus only, and we were in a completely different place than London. Different climate, different architecture. There are even palm trees there.

Cornwall is situated on the coast of Atlantic Ocean.

I liked this area of UK very much.

As soon as we had arrived to Plymouth first problem occurred. My mother couldn't find her luggage anywhere. That was terrible. Of course we I asked the driver about it, but he couldn't help us. I think he gave us a telephone number to call. Any way, it was never going to be found unfortunately.

We took a taxi from Plymouth to Perranporth, and somebody from this Care Home, I was going to work, picked us up, and took us to this accommodation provided.

It was a flat. I had left children with my mother there, and I found this Care Home I was going to work in. Boss showed me around. After that I had a look around Perranporth, which is a charming, little town. You can see the Ocean, and rocks from the town center.

'So that's going to be my new home' I thought to myself and smiled.

I was exhausted after this long journey from Poland to England. I think it took us at least 12 hours to get there. I was sure my mother, and children were very tired too.

First thing I did in this flat was to have a bath, and later on quickly I was in bed.

Then I heard a knock on the door. I opened it, and I was told by some man that we should leave this flat immediately, because I should have come to that work on my own. My children, and mother weren't welcome there. And of course I lost my job (not even starting it yet). It happened in the hours of afternoon. We were all forced to leave Perranporth, although we had just come from Poland, which is around 1500 miles from there, with two little babies of ours. It was too much to bear. How wicked it was. We couldn't even get one night sleep in this accommodation, to have a rest after this long journey. That was definitely unfair.

But we were just foreigners in a strange country. Nobody cared about us. You don't know the rules, so you brake them accidentally. And then you get punished without any mercy.

We didn't know back then how to rent a flat on our own. Besides I lost my job, so there was no point to stay in Perranporth any longer.

So we took our suitcases, and the other luggage, and we jumped on the train to Birmingham to stay at Patricaia's house. I still had her telephone number.

I will never forget this journey. My mother must have been so scared. I wasn't nice to her at all.

The problem was, that she wanted to come back straight back home to Poland, while I wanted to stay in UK no matter what. I was too close to make my dreams come true just to give up on them.

So we came back to Plymouth, and then we took a train to Birmingham, but not direct one. It was getting late. Everything was on my head. Kids, my mother's complaining, luggage. I just felt awful. Like never before. Going into unknown, dragging family behind me. This responsibility was about to kill me.

Nobody knew how it would all end. From this point of view, it didn't look like a happy end to me. It looked more like a disaster. If it wasn't disaster yet, it was going to happen.

It was dark, and we were still on the train. Conductor, who was checking the tickets, told us that we would have to get of the train in Bristol, because it wasn't a direct train to Birmingham.

We ended up in Bristol Railway Station basically in the middle of the night. There were no other passengers, waiting for their trains. After a few minutes we were stopped by same worker of this Railway Station, and we were told we couldn't spend the night in there with little children like that. So they ordered us a taxi to Birmingham, and it was going to be paid by them. We couldn't believe in that.

I hadn't called Patricia before. to warn her that we were coming. I know I should have done so.

We ended up in her house around three o'clock at night. Thank God she opened the door.

I explain her our situation. I introduced my mother to her, and children. I said sorry to wake her up at night like that.

She put us to sleep. We were safe. We could have some rest after our long, and exhausting journey, with unexpected turns.

Mother was complaining, because she didn't have anything from her necessary things to start the day with, like cosmetics, and clothes (her bag was lost on the bus to Plymouth). We didn't get it back.

Patricia again didn't let me down, which was good. She made me feel welcome at her house once more.

My mother started to arrange her journey back home. Father of course was helping her to get a bus ticket. She had had enough of this adventure.

I was very disappointed about that.

She'd given me the rest of pounds, and she was gone.

I knew Walsall a little bit, because I'd been there before.

For this money, my mother had given me, we did big shopping in Tesco with children (I mean grocery shopping). After this shopping I had no money left.

To make matters worse, the same shopping somebody quickly thieved in front of Patricia's house. I had left the bags for a moment on the pavement in front of the house, and I took kids to the house first (Pawel was in a pram). After a few seconds later my bags were gone. I was just shocked. That's how I was left with absolutely nothing. All I had was my children. Even Pawel's old pram from Poland was broken. I couldn't use it anymore. I had to carry him in my hands everywhere we were going.

My real struggle began. The only hope, that kept me going was that dream, that John would join us soon. But it was just a dream. I had no idea when it would happen (if it ever happen under these circumstances).

I had lost my job in Cornwall. For John to come I needed to get another job to do that registration with Home Office, I could send these documents to Jamaica, for John to get a visa to come to UK.

I even started to look for work in Walsall, but I couldn't stay longer in Patricia's house, because I had some problems with her husband Phill.

He just wasn't nice to me. Phill disconnected his house phone, because I was trying to use it. Things got out of hand. I didn't feel welcome in this house any more.

These problems with Phill reminds me of similar situation with my father. He didn't disconnect his phone, but he also was arguing with me, and John about his phone bill. We called Jamaica for papers to get married to John's family. That's why the bill was so high. When father saw the bill, he got mad.

Every one care only about themselves. Nothing else matters. When you go against your father's will, you cannot count on him any more. That's the truth, and it used to hurt before, but not anymore.

Besides I noticed, that in Poland no man is a good candidate for husband in fathers' eyes. John is black. That was even worse, because my father does not like black people.

I had never thought about racism before, but some people are like that.

They think they are better than any body else. It's just in their blood. They think that nobody else deserves life they have.

But they are wrong. All people are the same, and want to have in life the same chances.

When I was coming back from England to Poland by bus alone, when I had left my children with my family in Swinoujscie, I met one man on the ferry from Dover to Calais. His name was Jonas. Originally he was from

Nigeria, but he lived in London. We talk a little bit on that ferry. He even gave me his telephone number. I didn't know back then that I would ever need it.

The time came for me to call Jonas in Walsall. Only he could save me from Phill, Patricia's husband.

I called him from the nearest phone box, asking for help.

He told me to come to London with children, and call him when we get there.

I told about it to Patricia. She quickly bought us train tickets to London Euston. The same day in the evening they took us with Phill to the Railway Station, and put us on the train to London. She gave me thirty pence only to call Jonas from the phone box, when we get there.

One more time we were with children, and luggage on the way to the unknown. I had no clue what would happen next with us.

But I kept going, burning bridges behind me. There were definitely too many obstacles on my way so far in this strange country.

Would London be kind to us, or let us down, like the rest of these places in UK, or not?

In the space of a few days, I had lost so much. First of all I'd lost work, and accommodation in Cornwall. Later on my mother had left me. At the end I had lost my temper with Phill. Not to mention pram, shopping.

One thing I hadn't lost yet was a big hope to be reunited with my husband soon.

CHAPTER 5

I had never been to London yet. We were only just passing through two times with children on the way, and back from Jamaica. And also on the way from Poland to Cornwall we had been with children, and mother in Victoria Couch Station.

It's a city famous all over the world. Many tourist come to visit capital of Great Britain every year.

You can find there anything you can think of, like museums full of expensive, and very-well known paintings. Theatres, opera, you name it. There is of course House of Parliament called Westminster, many statues of famous people, Bank of England, a lot of very old bridges, palaces, parks and churches. There is River Thames, and a lot of modern skyscrapers. Not to mention shops, especially those on Oxford street.

London is, and always will be the place to be. Many students from UK, and from abroad come here to study in prestige Universities, and Colleges.

Young people, and adults, who come from different parts of the country, or the world try to make it in London.

There are many chances there to get a good job. People earn more than anywhere else, but prices in shops are higher. The same with rent, and cost of living.

Everyone is proud to be a Londoner. The society is very mixed. You can see here all nations, working together as one.

It was evening already, when we arrived to London Euston Railway Station with children. I had a lot of luggage, and two little children of mine to take care of. I had to carry Pawel in my hands all the time. I had left broken pram in Patricia's house.

Fortunately I got a good assistance from this railway station worker.

There was thirty pence in my wallet to make a call from a phone box to Jonas.

I did what I had been told to do by him. I called him, and he told me to get a taxi, and come to Brixton. He was in a pub there. He told me the name of this pub. Again I did, what I had been told to do by Jonas. Taxi driver helped me to pack my bags into the taxi, and we were on our way to Brixton. I was only hoping, that my friend would pay a taxi fare. It wasn't such a long journey.

I found Jonas in that pub, after we had arrived. He paid the fare, and helped me with bags, and the kids.

Another risky idea was put into action. Our fate was in hands of a strange man in a strange place.

It must have been so tough for John in Jamaica. I was calling him as much as I could from those phone boxes in England, to make him know what we were going through here. So he knew about Jonas.

But John wasn't better than me, and I was worried about him too, because he lived with his last baby mother, and their son, who was a little older than my Ewa in Kingston.

That almost killed me, when I was there with children to marry John. All these months I hadn't been aware about this fact, when we were apart. Not only I found out in Jamaica, that he had five children with three different women, but also I was told by John, that in his house in Sea View Garden he lived with Joanne, and their son Javier.

These news were shocking to me.

He swore he didn't cheat on me with her. We had been separated in different countries for ten months. That is a long time.

John just lived there, because he had nowhere else to go. Before he had been living with his aunt, but he didn't feel comfortable there.

It took me a few hard days to come to terms with these revelations, and to make my mind what should I do next.

I thought that it only is happening in films, drama like that, just before wedding. But unlikely it was my own drama.

After these couple of days, I made up my mind, and decided to believe John's version of events.

I had made this journey of my life over Atlantic Ocean for one reason, and one reason only to marry love of my life. Nothing couldn't have stopped me. I was on a mission, and I had to complete it.

Things I did in Jamaica, I would never do again.

At first John put us with children to stay in his brother's place in countryside, near town called Old Harbour. The reason why he did that was for us to be safe. In Kingston, where he lived, and worked was too dangerous.

I didn't like this place at all, and people who were there (John's brother Nicky, with his girlfriend, and their baby Crystal).

What was there to like? Not a thing, except neighbors, who were very curious, and friendly.

Nicky every day was fighting with his girlfriend inside the house.

There was no running water. How is it possible in 21st century?

No washing-machine.

I'd seen places like that on television, but till then I didn't know they were real.

But probably the worst of all was hot climate. You cannot escape it.

The only time to go out of the house was early morning 5-6 o'clock am.

I belong to people, who always like to go out. I don't like to be stuck in the house the whole days. My favorite reason to go out of my house is to do all kind of shopping. I also like to take children to the park, or just for a walk.

That's why I was so unhappy in Jamaica during this one month we were there. Tropical climate, and luck of money kept us inside for almost the whole time. John most of the days was nowhere to be seen. He worked and lived in Kingston. I did not see him a lot, which was heartbreaking to me. That wasn't the way I had imagined to be.

The only person, who was a little interested in helping me was John's aunt, called Auntie Vodney. She is his favorite aunt. She came to visit us with when we were staying at Nicky's house. Later on she helped John to rent us a room in Harbour View, close to the airport in Kingston.

Thankfully there was running water, and a washing-machine in this house. But there was only cold water in a pipe, and I wasn't allowed to use washing- machine.

At least in this house I knew a little bit what to do. I came back to my senses.

To be honest, a few first days in Jamaica I was very ill. I had another breakdown. It was connected with my mental illness. John didn't know how to help me. Nobody knew.

Besides anybody from my side of the world would feel bad.

I met a few people in Jamaica hungry, begging me for a little bowl of rice to cook for dinner.

Also people suffering, who couldn't afford medical care. Like this man with injured eye from the longest time couldn't afford X-rays.

Not to mention fights on the street of Kingston I witnessed with machete.

And before I was visiting John in Jamaica I had hoped to stay there forever. I even tore return plane tickets to Poland in John's presence to show him how much I loved him, and wanted to stay with my Jamaican man.

We got these tickets back in British Airways office a few days later, after John had explain to me, that it wasn't possible for us to live in Jamaica together.

I just didn't know then what I know now. I wish I never knew.

About that people can be hungry.

About that people suffer without an end.

About that people can be different than me.

And about that nothing can be done about it.

We couldn't make it in Poland, because John was deported from there.

We couldn't live in Jamaica, because it's a poor country.

That's why we could only find a refuge in United Kingdom.

It was hard for me, and children these first few months in England, but I deeply believed in what I was doing.

Of course I felt sorry for my children, although I did everything to protect them. Nothing bad happened. Thankfully.

Also thanks to Jonas. He helped me a lot. I know now, when I think about it.

Brixton is a place in London very popular among Jamaicans. It's quite close to the city center, about half an hour by bus. There is a big library in the center of Brixton, big market, and a lot of shops. I quite liked it there.

Jonas was Nigerian, from Africa. I don't have any contact with him any more

What he did was putting me with children for one night to sleep somewhere in Brixton. In the morning he told me what to do to get temporary accommodation for us.

I was so fool, because I gave him my wedding ring, and my diploma not to lose them. I was hoping to see him again, so he could give me them back, but it never happened. Back in the days I didn't know the value of the things. Some of them are irreplaceable, like weeding ring. John was so disappointed, after he had found out about it. He was the one to buy our wedding rings. We chose them together, when we were in Poland. I liked them a lot. Symbol of love.

Diploma was very important too to get a job. Later on I got a duplicate from my Medical College in Szczecin, in Poland.

Anyway, in the morning Jonas ordered us a taxi, gave me ten pounds, and said good bye. Taxi took us to Lambeth Housing Association in Brixton.

I didn't even know how this system operates.

Our luggage was outside this office.

I was trying to get for us some temporary accommodation.

Basically we were homeless with children for one day in November.

We waited the whole day, but it was worth it. In the middle of that waiting I took children to the nearest McDonald's, where I spent my ten pounds, given to me by Jonas. The last money again in my wallet. In the evening the decision on our fate was made. We were allocated a room in a hostel in Stretham. I didn't have a clue where was that. I was trying to catch a bus, but with children, and luggage it was difficult. Some black woman, seeing me struggling, gave me money for a taxi. We reached there around 5 o'clock pm. They were about to close the office, but luckily they let us in, and showed us our room. It was a big room on the ground floor, with three beds in it. We had to share a kitchen downstairs, and bathroom, which was upstairs.

I felt quite relief when I saw this room of ours in London.

CHAPTER 6

But somewhere to sleep was one thing, but what to eat, and how to feed my children was another. My very last money Jonas gave me I spent in McDonald's.

Our situation was hopeless. No money for anything, no one to turn to.

The same evening we'd got the place in that hostel in Stretham, when children were sleeping, I went out on my own to see what can be done to get some food.

Hostel is situated in the center of Stretham. There are many shops nearby, like Iceland, Lidl, even Polish shop is there, KFC, and of course off licence, corner shops, and Asian supermarkets.

I couldn't buy anything in those shops. I could only look hungry, and thirsty. There was no guarantee that my children, left alone, were still sleeping.

I was dying to call John, just to hear his voice. That was probably the worse thing: no money to call Jamaica.

Stress, stress, stress.

Desperation.

One idea came to another. What to do? Where to go? I was running out of time. Hunger could wake the children up anytime. I could lose them.

One homeless man somehow noticed me struggling, and gave me a piece of cold pizza. I think his name was Michael. I ate it.

I came back to my children. Thank God they were still sleeping. Nothing bad happened to them.

I couldn't wait for the morning to come. It came.

First thing in this morning I headed to the office in that hostel with children to ask for help. They wrote me a letter, and told me to take it to the nearest Job Center. This letter was about what I didn't have, and what I needed straight away.

To move around I needed pram for Adam.

I carried him in my hands all the way to Job Center in Stretham. Job Center is situated not far from the hostel.

To live I needed money for food. To cook I was in need of pots, glasses, cups, plates, cutlery, kettle. To sleep I required some blankets, pillows, sheets.

Just like a day before we had spent the whole day in Housing Association to get this temporary accommodation, we were waiting the whole day again in Job Center to get some money for the living. I got a cheque for over four hundred pounds. I cleared it in the nearest Post Office. It was about to be closed. I didn't have a bank account in England yet, so they gave me cash.

My relationship with is tricky, and it has always been. Money in my hands is like water. I spent quickly, and I don't think about tomorrow. Sometimes there is nothing left for essential things. When you are alone that's fine. Only you suffer. But when you have family it is disaster.

John hates me for this approach to money. We don't have any savings, and at a rate we are going, we will never have.

We don't own anything, although we are not that young any more. We live in Council house, and we own an old car.

I'm dreaming to get at least a small flat in the center of Walsall. I don't drive, so I am always like to be near the shops. John is dreaming about new car.

I have never had any contracts of employment yet in UK. John had had, but he lost this job, because his permit expired.

No cash, no chances for any mortgage, or loan from the bank. That's our life. From hand to mouth.

And that's all down to me.

When I was younger I wasn't very serious about this live. John is eight years older than me. Generally I didn't care about the money too much. That's the way I was. I gave up so many good jobs in Poland. One after another. I had had also one good pharmacy in London, which I gave up too after a few months. I have a good profession. I have pharmacy technician diploma. But somehow I was never settled at those jobs. One little problem appears, and I am looking for a way out of it. Something, which for anybody else would be nothing. Maybe it's connected with my illness, maybe not.

We were struggling many times, but I was never the one to be blamed for. I didn't feel guilty. John was working all these years to take care of us, while I was taking care of children, and the house. I didn't see anything wrong with that.

I was so happy when I got this cash in my hands. We went with children straight to Iceland to get drinks, and bread, and milk, and sweets. I will never forget delicious taste of tropical juice, after being thirsty the whole day in Job Center. I also bought a card to call John. I didn't need to beg for money any more to call him, which I had done before. Shame on me. But I just had to call him no matter what. There was a phone in the hostel, just in front of our room, so I didn't need to leave children alone any more.

I couldn't wait for another day to come, so I could buy the rest of essential things. It was the third day when I had to carry Pawel in my hands. I desperately needed pram for him to move around. I couldn't go on like this any longer.

Before I always had had very expensive prams, especially for Ewa, which was bought by my mother. It was such an exciting day in Swinoujscie. My mother was pushing empty pram through the whole time with me by her side. Father was then at work at sea, and John still in Switzerland. Of course the choice was mine, because I like to choose myself.

When Pawel was born one and a half years after Ewa automatically he took her space in her pram. She had to start to walk, but she wasn't ready for it yet. It had to be very hard for her, because she was just a litter girl. Ewa was used to sit comfortably in a pram, or sleep in it. Double prams weren't very popular back then in Poland. Second pram I owned was bought by father for Pawel. The same one, which broke down in Patricia's place.

The next day after I had got my first cheque from Job Center I took my babies to do this big shopping in town. First of all I got a nice, new pram for Pawel in Argos. It was navy blue, brand Chicco. I didn't have to carry him in my hands any more. Some women like to carry their children, but I don't belong to them. I liked to push my babies in the pram all the time, when I was in the streets. Buying this pram made me very, very happy. I quickly put Pawel in it in the shop. Later on I could continue to shop, I could hang shopping bags on this pram, or put them underneath the seat. I don't wish anybody to be without a pram even for one day, because it's just horrible. The same day I got for us some sheets, blankets, pillows, kettle, pots, plates, cutlery, glasses, cups, and even fancy lamp for children with fish inside. Ane more food. I told the woman from my hostel how much money I got, and what I bought for it. I think the were happy for me. I was told by one of them that I should have bought a cheaper pram from Argos, because soon I might not have money for food again.

Shopping is pure pleasure, but what to do in that room with my children was another thing. I just didn't have a clue. Taking care of the place were I live never come naturally to me. Cooking is the main activity in every household. Somehow I was trying to do that from one meal to another. Pawel was still drinking milk from the bottle. He turned one in that hostel. He made his first independent steps there. So I cooked whatever I could, and what I could afford. Cleaning is the next thing I'm not good at. I was doing my best, but, I am afraid, it wasn't enough. It's good that nobody was checking the state our room was in. Washing clothes I'd always liked, but it this accommodation washing-machine wasn't provided. Of course I didn't have television, or radio at the beginning.

I quickly started to make friends in that hostel. Most people who lived there were young. Especially I was close with sixteen years old, black girl called Terrina. She lived in a room next to us. She liked music, just like me. Sometimes I borrowed her radio, and CDs, I liked her. She was British, just like another black girl called Chantelle. She had had some problems with her boyfriend. She was forced to move out. That's why she ended up in temporary accommodation. There were some people from Somalia, but I didn't like them, and big woman from Nigeria. She was always using this phone in a hostel. She introduced me to this card to call abroad for only one pound. Sometimes, when I couldn't afford this card to call John, I used credit from her card without her permission. That was funny. I also called my parents from time to time. I just couldn't help myself. Everybody in this hostel was waiting to get a proper place to live like flat, or house. I was hoping to get a flat too one day.

CHAPTER 7

I didn't come to London to make friends. I came there to get a job, and papers to send my husband to Jamaica, to enable him to join us in UK. I was alone with two little children, so I needed first to find some nanny for them. My new friend Terrina seemed to like my children, so I asked her if she would like to take care of them, while I was away. She said 'yes'. So one problem was solved. I was happy about that. Of course I was going to pay her for that. I could start to look for a job. Job Center was the best place to start with. It wasn't difficult at all. One day I took part in Job Center in Brixton in interview, and I was offered a position of parking attendant in Kensington and Chelsea. I didn't even know what it was, and what my duties would be like. I was going to have two weeks training first somewhere in Central London, far from where we lived. Or course I quickly run out of money. Four hundred pounds, which I got from Job Center, couldn't last me forever. But I was hopeful. I was about to start a new job, and money should follow after.

I had nanny for Ewa and Pawel, but I didn't have money for transport to get to Kensington, where my training was going to be. Job Center didn't want to support me any more. No more crisis loan for me.

I was running out of time. There was only one thing left to do: to travel without a valid ticket.

Understandably I didn't know many places in London. When we first came to London Euston from Birmingham it was already dark. I didn't see very well our way to Brixton in a taxi that evening. On our way from Brixton to Stretham it was dark too. I don't drive, so I only know the way when I travel by bus, or on foot. When somebody is driving me I don't have to concentrate where we are going. It's always like that. I like to know where I am. I had been good with reading maps before sat-nav came. Just like I had been good at reading books, and magazines, which were replaced by internet. I cannot believe in a speed our world is going. Almost all aspects of life are different than they were before. I finished my education in 2001, and because I was a good students I thought I knew it all. I was sure I'd conquer the world. To be honest, I am completely lost in this twenty first century. Things I believe in are not important any more. I should be teaching my children everything, while they are the ones to teach me technology now. But when I am on my own I cannot help myself. It just me and mobile phone, or laptop and nothing cannot be done. I'm used to go to places to talk to people. But it's not possible any more in most cases. People are somewhere behind those screens of computers, and for somebody like me it's difficult to get to them for an advice. Passwords, usernames, log ins, emails, video calls, websites. That's the reality we live in now, which I don't like. Maybe I am old-fashioned. It's hard for somebody like me, but what about elderly people, who live alone, and have nobody to help them with technology? I cannot even imagine.

Job Center didn't give me a lot of money after all, so quickly I had to turn to food banks, and other charity place for clothes, and even the nearest St. Lawrence's Catholic Church for support with children. The nearest food bank from our hostel was in Brixton. It was far, particularly for Ewa, who only two at that time. But we had to eat. I never had money for bus fare, so we had to walk. Pawel was in his pram, so he was all right. Most of the things we were getting were tins like beans, spaghetti hoops, sausages. I had never eaten food like that before, when we were living in Poland. So it was hard to swallow these things. The best from them were sausages, because I was familiar with them. Sometimes we were eating them on the street on the way back to the hostel. Me and Ewa. Pawel was too young to eat sausages. I don't remember being hungry, but this fact proves that I was. And children must have been hungry too.

I was very worried about tomorrow. I just couldn't believe the position I put myself, and kids in.

The worse was to be in a grocery shops without money. I was seeing all these products I liked, but I just couldn't buy them. They were so close to me, but at the same time miles away, because I couldn't get them.

Food was one problem, but clothes was another. How to wash clothes without washing-machine? I had never been without washing-machine in Poland. There was a launderette nearby, but of course they charged for using their washing-machines, and you needed to have your own washing-powder. I didn't use this service at first. It was cheaper to get some second-hand clothes from the charity place, close to the hostel. I liked to go there. At least I had somebody to talk to. One woman from there helped me to open a bank account. I needed to open one to work in England. St. Leonard's Catholic Church was opposite to the hostel. We were attending church service every Sunday. One nun helped me to get some washing-powder to wash clothes one time.

Besides I also had my Gypsy friends, who were begging on the streets of Stretham for money. They weren't allowed to come to my hostel. People were afraid of them, that they would steal, but these girls were good to me. Before Christmas they brought me some food. Sometimes they were giving to me a pound, or two for cheap chocolates from Lidl. One of them was only sixteen. She wanted to become pregnant to get a flat.

Not to mention two shop owners I got involved with. One of them was from India, with a turban on his head. And another one from Pakistan. One evening this one from Pakistan took me to his car, and asked me how much money I wanted for sex with him. The other one even had my mobile number, and visited me in the hostel, and he wanted to kiss me. They got me wrong. I just wanted things from their stores, which I couldn't afford.

Jonas, the man who had helped me to get this room in a hostel, came to visit me once. He didn't give me back my wedding ring and diploma. I was hoping he could borrow me some money, but I didn't get anything more from him. I wasn't going to see him since.

John knew everything about these 'chances' with men. I'd never do nothing to hurt John. The reason I was in UK was to be reunited with my Jamaican husband.

That's why after all this hardship I was happy, and relieved when I got my first job in London. Just like anybody would be, I was full of hope, that our life with kids would improve, and John would be able to come to England as soon as possible.

I found out in the nearest library how to get to Kensington, where my training to become parking attendant was going to be. I got a map. I was ready for my first day of training except not to have money for a train ticket. But I had to go there. I had left Ewa and Pawel with Terrina, and headed to the nearest railway station Stretham Hill early in the morning to be on time. I managed to get there without a ticket. I used old tickets, which I had found on the floor. I had never done things like that before. Shame on me. I treated it like a kind of adventure. Everything was all right after first day of training. My trainer's name was Michael. I was making a lot of notes, and things like that. Parking attendants duties were to give penalty tickets to drivers, who didn't park their cars properly. We were told it was a dangerous work sometimes, because drivers didn't like to get these tickets. We were going to get an uniform, and a kind of walkie-talkies to have contact with the main office to keep us safe. I also came back to the hostel without a ticket, and without being lost. Children were well-taken care of by Terrina, so I was happy. But next day of my training was the last one. I was late. I didn't call Michael, because I didn't have credit to call from my mobile. He let me in, but in the middle of the day he simply said 'take your belongings and leave'. I was shocked. I didn't expect it to happen. A few weeks ago I had lost my first job in England in Cornwall, and the same thing was happening to me again. I was even crying on the way back to my hostel. I was alone, and nobody to turn to, no shoulder to cry on. I couldn't even pay Terrina for taking care of Ewa and Pawel.

They were going to pay me for that training, but a few days after I had lost that job I got a cheque from this company for zero pounds on it. My British friends from the street(alcoholics) advised me to go to the nearest CAB (it stands for Citizens Advice Bureau) to help me to get money for that one day or training. I went there with children.As usual they were very helpful. They had written a letter to my workplace on my behave, and aftera few days I got another cheque for the write amount of money. At least I could pay Terrina for childcare.

Money is one thing, but thanks to this job I got so wanted papers from home Office. I was registered with them. It happened just before Christmas. I was over the moon! I quickly sent them to John to Jamaica, so he could start apply for UK visa.

Just after I had my first Christmas with children far from home, and anybody. It was tough. At least I had children. We even could afford some cake. We went to church to watch Nativity. The most important thing, which kept me going, was that big hope in my heart that soon I'd see the man I loved.

CHAPTER 8

Last time I had seen John ten months before he came to England. We got married in Spanish Town in Jamaica on Saturday, and on Monday I was on my way back home to Poland with Ewa, and Pawel. It was heartbreaking to leave my husband behind. We didn't know when we'd see each other again. Everything was in my hands.

Although it was hard to get to that point, I was very proud of myself. We were with children in England, we had place to stay, and John was on his way. He got his visa at the beginning of January. I was so excited! He was ready to come. I even managed to buy for him a plane ticket from Kingston to London Gatwick airport. At first I didn't pay the whole price for it in this touristic office in Stretham. I persuaded this man to book that ticket for John without paying full charge, because I couldn't afford it.

Back then I could get away with everything. I couldn't afford this, or that. At the beginning when you live in a strange country you think you don't have to know the rules. But the rules are almost the same in almost every country. Without the money not much can be done. Deep down inside me I knew it, but I was just kidding myself. God will provide. God will provide those who provide themselves.

I wasn't the only one without husband by my side. I thought it was unfair that we were apart for such a long time. We were not the ones with John to be blamed. It was down to my parents, who didn't approve of my relationship. My parents had it all. Big house, their own business, while we only had our love. We used to live under their roof for a few months, after Ewa had been born. I was working in my mother's shop, while John was taking care of our baby. Father was all the time unhappy. I was using their kitchen to cook for us. Many times I was coming upstairs to John and Ewa with tears in my eyes, because of what father said. After a few months like that father told me that we couldn't live together any more. He was going to buy us a flat. It was sad to hear that. Very sad. But somehow it didn't happen. He wanted to buy for us the cheapest studio flat in Szczecin for forty thousand zlotych with broken boiler in it. When we went there with John, and Ewa to see it we were disappointed. Location of it was just horrible. Far on the outskirts of Szczecin. Most of the people there were using coal, or wood to heat up their flats and cook. I couldn't imagine to live in a place like that. So I refused it. Thank you daddy. We were living after that 'chance' another half of a year in my parents' house. At the end of this period John was deported to Jamaica, like a criminal, and wasn't able to come back to Poland for five years. John was coming back home from the pub drunk one evening. Father didn't let him in. John was obviously furious. He was shouting, and kicking the door. Father called the Police on him. John was taken to the station. They found out that he was illegal in Poland, because his visa had already been expired. That's how I was left alone pregnant, with Ewa, who wasn't even one year old yet. I couldn't stop the deportation although I had tried. It felt like it was the end of the world to me. John had been helping me with everything, and suddenly he was gone from our life. Of course I loved him, and couldn't imagine my life without him.

Love always wins at the end. My moment of glory was when we were going with children to pick up John from Gatwick airport without tickets again by train. It was at the beginning of February. We managed to get there without any problems. To see him at the airport was one of the happiest moment of my life, which I will never forget. My man was finally within my hands' reach. Immigration officer called me through megaphone. I had to confirm that I was the one to collect John from the airport. I was asked by him if we were married, and if I was working. Nothing could go wrong. John was shocked when we were coming back to the hostel by train without the tickets. We even got lost on the way, but I didn't care about that. As long as we were together we could be lost. Sometimes I am like that. I can find my destination, but I cannot find my way back. That's why I don't drive. It can even happen to me inside the building. Proudly I showed to John our room in a hostel. I don't know what he was thinking about it. It was quite messy. First thing he did was to clean the floor there. I am not very good in keeping place tidy unfortunately, and John doesn't like mess.

We had a lot catching up to do. John's cousin Patricia had told me before to start to take contraception pills not to get pregnant again. My mother should have told me that, but she didn't. It was a good advice. Before John came I had already started to take them. It's against teaching of Catholic Church, but I didn't have a better idea to stop from becoming pregnant for the third time. My mother is something else. She had never talked to me about sex, and things like that. Never ever. Before John I had had two boyfriends, but not a word from mother about sexual part of life, which exists. At school we had RE lessons with Catholic Priest. 'No sex before marriage'. 'Family is important'. 'Children should be brought up by both mother and father'. These lessons I learnt. These lessons I believed in, and I still believe. But sometimes it's difficult to put these believes in action.

'No sex before marriage'.

I hadn't been interested in sex with my first two boyfriends until John touched me for the first time. I will never forget this John's first touch on my waist, while we were climbing up the stairs in his sister's house in Switzerland on the day of our first meeting. Later on he hugged me from my back in her living-room. All I knew was that I would like more touches like that, and everything what was going to follow them. I was sure I couldn't lose that chance. It was like opening the whole, brand new world to me. The world of desire. I had never felt anything like that before. That's why I couldn't sleep in the night, which followed the day of our meeting. I kept thinking about what was going on with me. I was so into this Jamaican man, who I'd just met. I so wanted to see him again as soon as possible to check if the feelings I had for him were real. Thankfully we met again the next evening. He took me to his sister's house again. We were talking, drinking. Then we started to kiss. One thing led to another. We went upstairs to John's bedroom. One John's 'please', and I broke the rule of Catholic Church 'no sex before marriage'. Do I regret it? No, because if I had said 'no' at the beginning John wouldn't like me. From this very first moment till now I have always been saying 'yes' to my man. I know how important physical contact is to him. Every time we fight, and quarrel we made up in bed. Sex is always saving our relationship. And I read that made up sex is the best. I have to admit it, but sexual intercourse is important to me too. I got pregnant for the first time very quickly. Within space of four months. Next time again eight months after Ewa had been born. Every time I was surprised. John probably not, because he had been in several relationships before.

'Family is important'. John had not to believe in it long years. I think it's because he was let down by his mother as a baby. She didn't even register his birth in Registry Office. His grandmother did that. Father unknown. He was raised by his grandparents from the early days of this life. After their death, he was on his own living in many different houses. From one auntie to another. That's why he fell in love quickly to have family on his own. Somebody to love, and care about. But John had been changing women, and ended up with five children with three different women. I don't want to judge, but I wasn't used to men like that. In communist time in Poland most of the time was 2+2, two parents, and two children. Communists weren't into Catholic Church, but family was important. Family is like a little cell in a society.

'Children should be raised by both mother, and father'.

I strongly believe in it. Psychologists, teachers, therapists would tell you the same thing. Even people of different religious backgrounds would agree. Marriage is a sacrament, and should last 'till death do us part'. Children are fruits of love between husband, and wife. Both of them have responsibility to love and cherish them, because children are precious. In my opinion boys need father more then girls, and girls need mother more. I think like that, because boys will become man one day, and girls women. You have to set an example for your children. They won't be the same as parents, but you have to try, and teach them what is important in life, and what is not. Children should know the whole your life that they can count on you, no matter what they do, or say. You cannot just turn back on them.

I am lucky, because all my children are very close to me. They know me so well, and I love them too. I don't hide anything from them. John is sometimes so mad with me, because of that. I love Ewa, Pawel, and Emilia to bits, and I really don't know what I would do without them. My family means the world to me. Every day is different, and I am looking forward to it. John sometimes regrets that we have got no friends, but I don't need anybody else. Just five of us is enough for me. He is blaming me that fact, but I don't think it's only my fault. For example his cousin Patricia was inviting us for dinner many times, but we never went. The same example are our friendly neighbors. Besides when somebody is going to come to our house John is extra stressed. Most of people, who come to us are some professionals like health visitor, or Ewa's nurses. He is stressed, because he is obsessed with cleaning. I am not. John is also worried how I will behave, if I don't say too much, and things like that. He wants to be proud, not ashamed of me. He never invites any of his friends to our house. I even don't know his friends because of that. I can count on fingers of one hand how many people have come to our house so far. Maybe on two hands. These people are:

Gosia, who is Polish like me. Debbie, who is Pawel's friend's mother (they used to be in one football team together) . My parents visited us two times for a few days. From John's side: Margaret, John's sister from Switzerland, and her husband. And also John's brother from London. I must admit that all these visits were stressful to me. I just want everybody to feel well in my place. When I think about it I had never had many friends when I was at school. In primary school I had one friend, and in High School I also had one. My parents had to push me out of the house to go to playground to play. Especially I didn't like boys when I was in primary school. It changed in High School. I think I got on with boys better than with girls. I hated parties. There were a few birthday parties I went to. Most of them were 18th birthday parties. They were boring. Nothing interesting. Just a bunch of kids pretending to be adults, drinking, and smoking. I don't like to talk to too many people at one time. I like to talk to one person only. That's why parties are not for me.

I didn't like to be in a classroom full of students either. Too many people at one time. That's why I hated school although I was a good student always. One more thing I didn't like in my childhood were long trips away from home. They could last even three weeks. My parents were sending me against my will. Maybe they wanted to get rid of me. I only liked to spend the time with my mother, grandmother, and my auntie. My grandmother, and auntie Jola used to live around seven hundred kilometers from our place, so it's quite far. I visited them very often, particularly until the age of six, while I wasn't at school yet. They were the best for me. Auntie Jola even organized my christening in Church when I was around six. She took me everywhere with her. She was more like my best friend than auntie to me. I loved my grandmother too. We were playing cards together, and other games. She often visited us. Grandmother loved to travel. She used to take me for long walks. We were going to Church together. She taught me how to pray on the rosary. Sadly both of them are already dead. Auntie had died before grandmother. I didn't even attend their funerals, because of lack of money.

John often reminds me how he gave up contacts with his family to please me. It doesn't please me at all, but the same happened to me as well. When you live abroad, far from your loved ones it's difficult to stay close to them. People, who live in different countries don't understand one another. Problems, and challenges we face in England cannot be compared to those in Poland, America, Jamaica, or any other country. The longer you stay abroad, the more distant you are from country of your birth. I feel settled in UK from the longest time. I know that this country is definitely the best place for my family. Children are happy here. It wasn't always like that. In Poland, for example, they didn't feel comfortable being mixed-race in white people's country. It's surprising, but a little darker skin complexion can make a big difference to them, and people around them. There was nobody to relate to in Poland for me, and for my children. I didn't know anybody involved with a black man, and Ewa, and Pawel didn't see anybody, who looked like them.

In Black Country people are mixed. It's good for us. I noticed that although we are mixed as a nation, we stick to people of the same background. Black people tend to talk to blacks. Asians are friendly with other Asians. White people prefer company of other white ones.

I don't think too much about the colors of the skin, but I know one thing for sure that I am always attracted to black men. So our relationship with John was meant to be. I believe in that. My children are beautiful, I am proud of them, and I hope they know that, and they think the same about themselves.

I don't know about other black men, but John sometimes feels sorry for himself. On one side he is confident, but on the other he blames the color of his skin for bad things that happens to him. How many times I've already heard from him the sentence, which begins 'because I am black'. When it comes to treatment from my parents he got it's true. All this disrespect took place, because John is black. That is called racism.

Poland is a kind of racism country, I'm afraid. Not all polish people are like that, but bad things towards foreigners happen. Most of foreigners in Poland now are from Ukraine. There are black people in big cities, who are students, but not so many of them. That's why polish people are against them, because they don't know them. They hardly see them.

Of course there is no excuse for being racist. People are the same, with the same needs. No matter how they look like. You don't have to like anybody, but everyone deserves respect.

The worst possible situation is when foreigners, who live in a strange country forget where they come from. You have to always remember about your roots. For instance Pawel is ashamed to speak polish. He was born in Poland, he was going to reception there, but now he would rather hide this fact. Ewa doesn't have problem with that. She even did her exam GCSE in polish. Maybe he doesn't want to stand out. He should be proud of being bilingual, but he is not. Or my friend Gosia from Poland, who lives in England is against refugees coming to UK. She is a foreigner herself. She got her chance, but she doesn't think, that other foreigners deserve their chances too.

I'm not interested too much in what's going on in Poland now. I just talk to my parents. I'm interested what's going on with them only. My brother Thomas have two children. One from previous marriage, and the other one with his current wife, who I didn't meet yet. Two sons. At the beginning I was furious with him for what he had done.

In my opinion it's stupid to split up. Everybody has some reasons to do so, but I don't believe in that. Person, who wants to come out of a relationship, or marriage is looking for an easy way out. In a new relationship the same problems will appear sooner' or later. My brother cheated on Maria.

In my life I did everything I could to save my marriage. And also it was very important to me for my children to have father in their life. I know I was right.

It's very difficult to raise children on your own. For me it was harder to do that, because of rejection from my parents. Thankfully I didn't have to do that for a long time.

John can do everything in the house, so I am the lucky one. That's how most of Jamaican men are. Independent not to rely on anybody to do something for them. Most of these things John even does better and quicker than me. I have to treasure him. He is my big treasure, and I will never give up on him.

CHAPTER 9

Just before John came, I had got a job in the nearest KFC. John had already been with us when I started to work there. He was staying with children, while I was at work. I was doing mostly evening shifts. I was coming back to the hostel late, but it was very near (ten minutes walk). Every evening I was bringing some free food from my work place.

We weren't hungry any more. We didn't need to go to food bank any more, which was good.

John quickly adapted to life in Britain. It was so good to have him back. I was very, very happy.

I didn't like this job I KFC. Most of the time I was frying chicken, and cleaning, which I don't like to do.

I was so happy when I managed to find another job in pharmacy in Balham. I lasted in KFC about six weeks only.

Times were different before. Now it's difficult to look for work, because everything is online.

Before I found this job offer in the machine in Job Centre. I printed it out. There was an address of this pharmacy. I went there to ask what should I do to apply for this vacancy. I got an application form. I fulfilled it. A few days later I took part in an interview. And then I got a job.

Nowadays internet is everything, and nobody can escape it. Even a jobseeker. Thanks to my children I am good with laptops, computers, or smartphones. Everything I've learnt from them. But not always was like that. In 2010 we didn't even have a laptop, so I didn't know how to use it. Ewa, and Pawel had homework set up on Education City on internet, so we had to go to the nearest library to use computer to do it. Every Saturday we used to go there. It's good that it was close to our house.

School was one thing, but my job search was another. And of course internet was involved. First step was to create my cv. I could write in English, but I wasn't confident enough to do it myself. John sent me to one place in Walsall Town Center called JobChange. I made an appointment with an adviser. He took all relevant information from me, and my cv was ready to collect next week. This place was also very helpful with searching job online. I kept coming back there to use computer to look for job.

I was quite pleased with my new job in pharmacy in Balham. Every morning I had to walk to my work place through the park. I took me about half an hour. I was assisting pharmacist with dispensing medicines to the customers. It was an important role to do. John was still taking care of our children, while I was working. Sometimes even on my break we were meeting up on the playground in that park, which was nice. Pharmacy was closed for lunch break an hour and a half every day. We had to leave pharmacy for that time. Sometimes it caused problem to me, because I didn't know what to do during that break, and where to go. Pharmacy was situated in the town center. I never had any spare money to go to the shops with. I ate home-made sandwiches on the bench when the weather was good. The rest of my time I was spending in the library, reading magazines. I didn't like these lunch breaks at all. Manager could stay in the pharmacy during that time, but not the workers, which was strange, and unfair.

Our life in a hostel was good. We didn't have any television, or radio at first, but after a few weeks we managed to buy them. John wasn't unemployed a long time. He quickly found evening job in two surgeries to clean them. So we had extra money to spend.

Children were healthy, and growing fast. We often were taking them to the nearest park, so they could play.

I missed Poland a lot during that first year in Great Britain. I must admit that. Not only people, but also places like beach, promenade in Swinoujscie, and parts of Szczecin as well. I think it's natural to feel like that. Not all memories were bad from my country after all.

I was trying to hide that longing from John. But when our very first Easter came I couldn't hide it no more. I was just sad. I couldn't stop thinking about traditions we had in Poland, and food, made by my mother. I couldn't cook these special meals, and bake this yummy cakes.

Nothing specialtook place that Easter. I didn't even remember going to Church. John is not a big fan of Church, but I love going to Church. I wanted my children to know what their religion was. I remember Pawel one day when he was in primary school asked me if we were Muslims. A lot of his mates from this school were Muslims, and we didn't go to church so much. Sadly he just didn't know what his religion was. Now he knows, but he still doesn't go to church with us. Last time he went it was two years ago. But I will never give up to send him to Church.

All of this it's my fault only, because I didn't take Ewa, and Pawel to Church that much. It was about half an hour walk from where we lived before. We had to climb back the hill. Most of people from that Church were driving, so it was easer to get there.

At the beginning I didn't know how to behave in English Catholic Church. I was familiar with Polish Church in my country. Here I had to learn prayers, and order of the Mass in English language.

Now I am quite used to these Masses here, but it wasn't easy.

My friends from the hostel were getting flats one after another. They were moving out of the hostel. We were waiting to get a flat too. I didn't know how this system was working, but every day I found out something new. There no possibilities like that in Poland with social housing. People in Poland have rent privately, or get a mortgage for the flat from the bank.

I'm not surprised that people from all over the world want to come to Great Britain to live.It's like a promised land for many foreigners. Help is here with money, housing. Schools are free of charge. NHS is taking care of anybody, with medicines free for many. There are a lot of benefits here, but the longer you live in this country the less you appreciate of what you get. You just quickly take things for granted.

Every country is different with different possibilities. But I didn't see them so many in Poland for my family, while we were living there. Not to mention Jamaica, where you have to pay for every appointment with the doctor, and every medical treatment, which is terrible. When you are sick, and poor you don't have a chance to get better. In Jamaica you also have to pay for going to school. Jamaica used to be British colony, but not any more. Now it's an independent country.

John is proud to be Jamaican. It's a proud nation. I have already met his three brothers, and two sisters. I got on well only with his younger sister called Tamara. We met in Switzerland. She is easy to talk to. With Margaret we don't have much in common. I spent in her house a few weeks, but we didn't talk too much. She is always busy working, cooking, cleaning, throwing parties. I belong to people who are quiet, and she is not like that. You cannot get well with anybody, can you?

I'm happy that I had a chance to meet all those people. I know that John is not the only one. I haven't met his mother yet. She lives now with Tamara in New York. Tamara has one child.

My children only have one set of grandparents from my side, which is a shame, but that's the way it is, and we have to accept it.

My parents are good when we need some help with money, but when it comes to children they are no good. Just after Ewa had been born, my mother was working, and after work she was cycling to the allotments to plant flowers, and vegetables. She didn't have time for us at all. Before I hadn't seen anything extraordinary in that. I thought it was normal.

John came, when Ewa was two months old. He didn't comment on my mother's behavior. He probably didn't want to hurt my feelings. After my father had come from work at sea the situation was even worse. He asked John one time 'why baby with no money?'. They weren't happy for us to have Ewa. John says, because Ewa was black.

We could count on ourselves only, when it comes to taking care of Ewa. The same problem I had after Pawel had been born. He was born in Szczecin, a hundred kilometers from Swinoujscie. My mother with Thomas collected us from the hospital. They did the necessary shopping for me, and they were gone. I didn't cope well the first night with Ewa, and new born Pawel. Both of them were crying. I had cesarean section with Pawel too. I didn't know what to do. I prayed to God to help me. And he did, while my mother was comfortable in her bed, while she should have been with us that night.

We can only count on ourselves, when it comes to our children with John only. We are used to that after all these years. We never go out on our own. We don't do dates, or holidays together. I know what we are missing out, but we never have anybody to stay with our children. I wish things can be different, but we cannot change them now. You cannot force people to do, what they don't want to do. As simple as that. On the other side you need that quality time with your husband for relationship to go in the right direction.

At home it's always about every day like what to do, what to eat, or where to go. We are lucky with John. We have never had any major problems with our kids. So far so good. Only Emilia doesn't listen to us at all, but maybe she will grow out of it (I am kidding myself).

I am not complaining about my life with John. I know that one day when we are older Ewa, and Pawel will probably move out. We will stay with Emilia, who is five now. Maybe then we will do together, only three of us, things we've never done before. For now we just have to take care of each other to live long to see these days.

I always tell John that life is long, and we have a lot to look forward to. I don't know if he believes me, or not.

Now when I am in my forties I feel happy. I don't think anything is missing from my life any more. I have three children (which is enough), good husband. I have somewhere to live, and a car to move around.

Before I always felt sorry for myself. Always something was missing from my life. I had Ewa. She was born, but John was missing. He wasn't with us when our first daughter was born. When Pawel was born John from the longest time had been in Jamaica, so he was missing again. In England at the beginning almost all necessities were missing like food, drinks, and even for one day somewhere to live.

Money was always an issue. John was telling me that he was earning enough, but I didn't see that. As far as I was concerned, from my point of view money was always tight. I just kept seeing things at home about to finish, and I was worried how to replace them.

John could do without many essential things, but I couldn't. I wasn't used to being poor. When I don't have what I usually use I'm mad. I don't like to use something else instead when I know perfect product is just within my hands reach(in the supermarket), and it doesn't cost a fortune.

In the house we used to live before there was almost everything old. Windows were old. Wind was blowing through them. Our boiler was old. We used gas to heat up the house, and to cook. We kept charging gas card as much as we could, but it wasn't warm in the house, because of those windows. We didn't have enough money to do that. John was getting paid at the end of the week on Thursdays. In the middle of the week I was always hoping, and praying that I would have enough gas to cook dinner to the end. I didn't work long months, while living there, so I was staying at home most of the time in bed, under the duvet, because it was very cold anywhere else. Things like that you would rather forget, but I remember that heat was missing from our previous house. But what can you do? You live somewhere, and it's hard to move out. Deep down inside you feel it's wrong. People usually don't live like that.

Everybody wants the best for their kids, but our life in Pleck wasn't the best. I never complained, but we both with John knew we could better. Things, and comfort might be missing from time to time, because circumstances change, but if good values are gone, and you don't cherish your life with person you love that's it. It's time to move on, and start all over again.

We've come a long way with John. We've had our ups, and downs, but we've never given up on each other. We have strong bond, and I hope nobody will never break it. Nobody, and nothing. However I feel (good, or bad) I am always proud of this fact.

So I am not sorry for myself any more. I know now that no matter how much money you have, if you don't save, your money will be finished one day. I was a specialist in spending all money I have access to in one day. No matter if it was ten pounds, or a hundred. I was always back home with nothing. And I was surprised when John got mad with me, because of that. I thought I wasn't doing anything wrong, and that I was innocent.

Life can be full of surprises. But I am like that. I'm always sure that nothing bad can happen to us. I'm optimistic. But shit happens, and on those unexpected occasions you need some money. For example for a taxi to go to the hospital, and things like that. Every adult knows that. That's why probably I felt so bad, because most or the days I was at home without money. Even if there would be any emergency at school with children, I wouldn't be able to help them, because I was stuck at home without money.

Sometimes I think that being dependent on your husband when it comes to money keeps couple together. I am dependent on John with money, but on the other side he is dependent on me with different things. I always do all paper work, calls, emails, and I keep in touch with kids' school. It's also important.

Work is hard for somebody like me. Always something is wrong. I don't need additional contact with people. I am happy staying at home, taking care of children and the house. I hate being far from home long hours, not knowing what's going on there. I feel like I'm lost forever. Maybe that's why I've been sacked so many times already from so many jobs. I learn quickly, that's for sure. I like to face new challenges. I'm punctual. But it meant nothing to my employers.

To be honest, I've never had a feeling yet that I was actually good in what I was doing in my jobs. No matter what kind of work it was, and where. I do my best, but my best is not good enough. There were so many dramas in my life losing one job after another. It's not a nice feeling. My hopes were high when I got them. John always was involved driving me to those places, and buying me things, which were required to start these jobs. All of them ended bad. That's why I am tired to try again, because obviously there is no chance for me to be settled in one of them.

Because I'm most of the time at home I'm close to my children, and they are close to me. Nobody can take that away from me. I adore them. I'm trying to be a good mum. Sometimes I might fail, but most of the time I'm good. I know a lot about them, and they know a lot about me. They never let me down. No problems at all with them.

Ewa, and Pawel are big now, but they still need me. Slowly they are becoming more, and more independent. I'm with them every step on the way. Ewa is brave, and she can talk to people without any problems. Pawel is shy. Very often he is telling me to be good to people, when I get mad at somebody.

Emilia is our baby girl, and she always will be. She has brought light into our family, which still shines. At the beginning I was struggling when she was born. John helped me a lot. He was the one to wake up at nights to feed her. Pawel didn't want another sibling, but now they are with Emilia best friends. Maybe I'm not good with newborn babies, but now when she is going to primary school I am the one to help her with everything. Everybody knows that it's important to do well at school, because it's benefiting students in the future. They have better chance to get a good job, and have a good life.

Unfortunately it's not always like that. Sometimes students, who do well at school struggle as an adult. Like me, for example. I was a good student in High School, but I wasn't offered places in Universities (I wanted to study English language, later on Polish). Finally I did pharmacy course in Medical College, and that is my occupation.

I could only do work well in Poland in my mother's herbal shop, and in community pharmacies. I also had one job in hospital pharmacy in Szczecin. My psychiatrist back then was surprised that I could work without any problems.

It's been twelve years since my diagnosis of bipolar disorder. I'm doing well now. I see psychiatrist from time to time. I am glad that I feel better than before. I'm more lively, and active most of the time. I still have my bad days, when the mood is low, and I don't have the strength to come out of bed in the mornings. I eventually always come out of bed for the sake of children, and John. I don't want them to be worried about me. John doesn't trust me, because of this illness. I can be unpredictable. It must be hard for him sometimes.

But not all the time. I can be nice to him too. When he is complaining about life with me, I always remind him, that he is the one to call me the first day we met. He cannot deny it. I'd never do nothing to hurt him. I'm doing my best to keep our relationship going. After all these years together we know each other very well. We quarrel very often, and every time it's about the money. I am ashamed of myself always. I don't want children to witness that. But there's nothing to be done about it.

John is like that: 'I am not cooking today', and a minute after he is in the kitchen, or 'I am not going anywhere today' and next thing he does is to have a shower, and put on his clothes to leave the house.

I believe in what people say. Every word has a meaning. Maybe that's why we have these arguments all the time. Sometimes he doesn't even remember what he says, and I have to remind him the words that hurt me so much.

These arguments are better than not to be able to be together. That's why I am so grateful to UK to give us a chance to be together again with John. This separation was unnecessary, and it lasted too long.

CHAPTER 10

In the middle of summer we got our big chance! After around nine months living in the hostel in Stretham my family got two bedroom flat in Sydenham. We found out about it through the letter from Housing Association. We were over the moon! Life in this hostel wasn't bad, but the less you share with strange people the better for you. We had to share kitchen, and bathroom with other tenants. Sometimes it caused tension between us. I mean arguments. Everybody's lifestyle is a little different. Especially mine, because I come from foreign country, and I wasn't used to English reality. There were also a lot of foreigners from Asia, or Africa there. Their culture is even more different. At least Poland is in Europe, and Asia, and Africa are on different continents.

When you live close to many people you tend to share stories from your life with them. John doesn't like people to know too much about our family (that's why probably we don't have friends). As far as I am concerned we have nothing to hide, but I just always want to please John, so I keep my mouth shut. My husband is my friend. I don't want to lose him, because of some other people. I cannot take that risk. Besides children are, and always will be my friends, so I have enough of them.

In that letter from Housing Association there was an appointment to see this flat first. A few days later we all took a bus to Sydenham to see the place., where we were going to move into soon. We were excited! It was quite far from Stretham. We were about to start a new chapter in our life. Life couldn't be better. The person, who was showing us this flat was a Jewish man. It was on the first floor in two-stores building. It was situated opposite to big supermarket called Saintsbury's, and the bus stop. On the ground floor there was a corner shop, Jamaican restaurant, and bakery. I liked it, and John liked it too. There was like a big balcony in front of the flat. Perfect for children to play, and for me to hang wet clothes. There was washing-machine in the kitchen, and other furniture. To see that washing-machine was a relief to me. Finally we were going to be able to wash our clothes in civilized way. Before we had had to use public launderette, which was hard. There was no such thing like washing-machine in our hostel. The man explained to us how to charge electricity, and gas using pre-payment card, and key. Or course we accepted the place. We were very, very happy! We could move in anytime, because we had the keys.

I was still working in that pharmacy in Balham. It's close from Stretham, but far from Sydenham. After we'd moved in(John took care of everything while I was at work) I had to find my way to work. I had to take two buses to get there. My manager, after he'd found out about our move, let me start work a little later than others. That was nice of him. He was trying to make my life easier. That could only mean one thing that he was pleased with my work.

John was still doing his two cleaning jobs in those surgeries. I managed to get a place in nursery for Ewa in the nearest Adamsrill Primary School. She was three years old then. I started to go to playgroup with children in the same school. We all enjoyed these sessions. There were nice toys there, and other children to play with. I was able to talk to the mothers of those children. I didn't talk to many of them. I made friends with Chinese sisters there.

In the meantime we had visitors from Poland. My brother came with his friend for the summer. They stayed in our flat. Thomas even got a job. He was delivering Chinese food for the nearest Chinese Restaurant. They spent only a few weeks with us.

I got an annual leave from work in the summer. We could go to visit my parents in Poland for the first time since we'd left. I was very happy about that. We took a bus from

Victoria Couch Station in London to Szczecin in Poland. John took us to the station, and we said good bye to him. The journey takes almost twenty four hours. We were excited to make it with children.

It was good to see my parents again. We spent there around two weeks. The weather was good. We were going to the beach, for walks on promenade, and riding bikes to Germany.

We had a good time in Poland, but it was also good to be back home. John picked us up from Couch Station. He was happy to see us.

I never returned to that job in pharmacy. The reason why was, because John got a good welding job, and I had to take care of our children. His job was better paid than mine. I never even informed my manager that I was leaving, which wasn't good. I don't know why, but I almost always burn bridges behind me, when it comes to my work places.

Ewa started her very first nursery in primary school. My duties were to carry her to school, and to bring her back. I was taking care of the house. Pawel was too young to go to school, so he was always with me. I didn't miss work at all.

Life was good. For the first time I felt settled in England. It took me almost two years to feel like that with many obstacles on the way. Many things happened, which shouldn't have happened to me, and children. I never knew that I'd be hungry, thirsty, and homeless in this country. I never knew that I'd be begging for money in the street just to make a phone call. Ewa had to walk such a long distance to get some food from food bank with me, and Pawel in a pram. Stories like that I'd known before only from books, and films until they happened to us. When I was experiencing all these bad things I couldn't believe it was happening to me. But I couldn't give up. I had to carry on, because I so wanted to be reunited with my lovely husband.

I don't know if I was right, or wrong. Love is like that. That's why people in love do whatever it takes to simply be together. Some people are lucky. They don't need to sacrifice anything. They just meet, fall in love, propose, get married, and live happily ever after.

We weren't so lucky with John at the beginning of our relationship. For some reasons nothing could be done. We wanted to live in Switzerland first, but I got pregnant, and I couldn't afford private healthcare in this country. In Poland we were persecuted by my parents. In Jamaica only one thing could be done: to get married, and nothing else.

That's why Great Britain for my family is the place to be. I have never been happier than here. I cannot imagine my life somewhere else.

John tends to complain about things, which are happening in here. Even today I heard from him that Jamaica is the best country. I know it's not. He might miss Jamaica, but most people from his family is somewhere else, so what to miss? His sister from Switzerland visits Jamaica regularly, and she says that people there still suffer. Not all of them of course.

When you start to live in foreign country you try to fit in as soon as possible. You observe people around you, and you try to copy them. Everywhere is a little different. Fashion is different, lifestyle, and culture. The reason why English people have their manners is down to Royal Family. They set an example for ordinary citizens, and it works. Queen Elizabeth The Second is a hard working person although she is in her nineties. She is married to the same man. A lot of women can relate to her. The same with Kate Middelton, and prince William. They have three children together. To me, and many other people they are like role models.These people build relationships, and they don't want to destroy them. They are getting stronger, and stronger, more, and more powerful among people all over the world. They even go to Church, which is not common, especially among young people. I really admire them, and many other celebrities couples, who are faithful to each other, respect each other, and stay together in love for ever.

Couples, who fight always lose. If I was independent maybe I would think different about our relationship with John. Or if I wasn't a Christian. Or if we didn't have children together. But I'm stubborn to stay by his side although he is not the easiest man to deal with. The problem is that people never change. All we have to do is to embrace them the way they are. We don't know how people feel. We only know how we feel. John is not good at explaining his feelings to me. He likes to stay at home all the time, and he is struggling to understand why I like to go out of bed early in the mornings. It's my life. Every evening I plan the next day. What to do, what to wear, and what to cook. I get up quite early, have a shower, get dressed, and I'm ready for the day. I like these mornings of mine. Emilia wakes up the same time as me, She sleeps in our bedroom. I try to go with her downstairs, where our living-room is, not to wake up John. We spend mornings with Emilia. I try to teach her a little bit of writing, and reading. In John's eyes what I'm doing in the house, and out of it's a waste of time. He thinks house work, and taking care of children is nothing (like a joke). I know I'm busy doing that, so he should appreciate it. The most important thing is to keep children safe. We used to fight with John, but children have never been hurt.

After a few weeks of John's work in Forest Hill we managed to buy a car. John didn't have to take a bus to work any more. We could do shopping, and go to different parks by car. A lot of people might think that it's normal to have somewhere to live, and car to move around. But to us these things were a kind of special, because of what we had been put through. John had had many cars in Jamaica, and even in Switzerland. He came to Poland by car, but we had to sell it later on. Men have special bond with their cars. Cars mean a lot of them. John even claims that he doesn't like to drive any more. It's strange. I can imagine this headache with parking, fixing, cleaning, tolls, congestion charge zones, and tickets. Bu still...I think he only says that, because he doesn't want to take us places. He likes to drive alone.

When I'm with him in the car it's like holidays to me. He obviously doesn't feel the same. I'm used to that now, but it still hurts. I cannot drive although I have a driving license. I think that's good, because I can get lost easily when I'm walking, or taking a bus. Even in the middle of the building it can happen to me, for example in hospital, or shopping center. When I am in unknown place I have to be very careful. That's why I like to go to places I know rather than the unknown. It's quite scary to be lost, especially when I am with children. With kids you should always know the way to lead them. If you are lost they are last with you too. I like to walk, and take a bus. Ewa, and Pawel are used to walking with me, but Emilia is almost always complaining. She would like to go by car everywhere. John never walks. Even to corner shop he goes by car. Some people are going for healthy walks, but not us, which is a shame. When we first met in Switzerland John promised to me to walk from Lausanne to Geneva along the shore of Geneva Lake. I liked that idea, but it never happened. He just doesn't like to walk any more. He used to play football when Ewa, and Pawel were younger with them a few years ago, but not any more. Somehow he became very lazy. Sport is good for everybody. My children like sport. At least they know what to do in their spare time. It keeps them awake from wrong friends, parties, and things like alcohol, or cigarettes. They've always been good kids, and I hope it will continue like that. I'm setting them good example, because I'm not interested in drinking alcohol, or smoking cigarettes. I don't go to parties.

My only regret, when it comes to bringing up my children Ewa, and Pawel, is not to teach them too much about our faith. I find it very helpful in my life, and I wish it was in theirs as well. But it's not. They don't pray. They go to Church occasionally with me. I don't know if it's my fault, or not. I have always kept the joy of prayer to myself. Sometimes they were praying with me, but that was a long time ago. Now I'm teaching Emilia how to pray.It's hard, especially in multi religion country like Great Britain, to keep children on the right path. Even recently Ewa was in the hospital again suffering another psychotic episode. I tried to introduced her to rosary prayer to St. Mary, my favorite one, but she wasn't interested. Pawel goes to Catholic School, but the subject he hates the most is RE. In my opinion faith helps you to make the right choices in life, particularly when you are young. Now when Ewa, and Pawel are crossing the threshold of adulthood I cannot help them any more. I cannot tell them what to do. They have to choose themselves. What if they will make the wrong choices? That's what I'm afraid of. The only hope is Emilia. Maybe soon she will start to love God like I do.

When I was a teenager I didn't have it easy when it comes to my faith. Poland is a catholic country, but my parents, and my younger brother didn't go to Church. Only on special occasions like Easter, or Christmas. I was the only one to go to Church every Sunday, and I liked it. It wasn't appealing to the rest of my family. It's like that up to this day. I get the impression that they are laughing at people, who go to Church including me. I understand not to go to Church, but to laugh at Catholics attending the mass it's not right. That's why it was difficult to me, because what I was doing all these years wasn't accepted by my parents, while I wasn't doing anything wrong. My grandfather (my father's father) also was close to God, and Church. When I first met John my grandfather asked me if John was Christian? That was important to him, not the color of his skin. John is Christian, but he doesn't go to any Church. He was raised by his grandparents, who were close to Church. His grandfather even was a pastor. John talks about God almost every day. But most of the time he does that when it's on news some disaster like flood, hurricane, or fire. He says 'Almighty is punishing people' like he was happy that disaster is happening to people. Like he is above it all. I never like that, because God I know is good, not wicked, and wishes people well.

Children might not know that yet, but at some point of life we are completely alone. We don't know what to do. Who to turn to for help. Bur Christians always know that God will help them. I don't wish them that, but it will happen sooner, or later in their life, and they should be prepared for that.

I remember when Ewa was ill for the first time. She was experiencing her first psychotic episode. The staff of PAU ward in Manor Hospital was trying to move her to psychiatric hospital for children in Birmingham. She was in such a bad state that she didn't trust anybody. Special transport was arrange for her by the hospital, but she wouldn't come inside this car. They wanted to put her back to PAU ward, but I had an idea that I would go with her. She trusted only me. So they agreed to that. I didn't have a lot of money. I didn't know where we were going. I was scared. Fortunately transport went well. Ewa was in the right place for her (The Priory hospital in Edgbaston). After we saw the doctor I was free to leave her there. It was after ten o'clock pm. No network connection on my mobile with ten pounds in my wallet. I didn't know how to come back home. These are moments I'm talking about we need God's guidance when we simply don't know what to do. It was a kind of adventure. I found a bus to Wolverhampton on the high street, and from there I took a taxi back home (John paid for it).

But the other times can last long when we don't know for example what career to choose, or who to fall in love, or you name it. I just wish my children were prepared for that. I'll help them as much as I can, but I'm sure my help won't be enough. Ewa, and Pawel could find a relationship with God themselves. They are too big to be pushed into it. They have never had a boyfriend, or girlfriend yet. I hope they won't fall in love with person with different religion. Just like John's cousin Patricia's son converted into Muslim to be with his Muslim wife. That would break my heart if it happened to my children. I even know him myself. He is a good son to Patricia, but he is living in different world than she. She respects his choice. She has never complained about that to me. But if it happen to me, I'd be very disappointed.

People in Britain get married late, and they have children later thanit was in my times in Poland. They want to have career first, own a house, have some savings, and then thinking about having children. That's not such a bad approach, but a lot of women in their thirties, or forties cannot get pregnant. A lot of them turn to IV treatment to get pregnant, which is expensive (especially when you have to try many times). This fact can put pressure on relationship.

When you are younger it's much easier to get pregnant. Maybe you don't have any savings, or you rent a house, but you are a happy mum without spending fortune on IV treatment.

And one more thing I noticed bringing up my three children. When you are younger you have more strength, and heart to take care of your kids. It was like that when I have Ewa, and Pawel. When Emilia was born I was thirty nine years old. I was thinking to myself 'she will make us with John feel younger than we are'. But it wasn't like that at all. John had to help me with her a lot although it was my idea to have this baby.

In our Sydenham flat we spent our first Christmas together from the longest time. On Christmas Eve we were stuck in our broken car somewhere in Central London for a few hours. We even didn't have our shopping done for Christmas. Eventually someone helped us to move the car. We came back home late. But we were together. That what mattered the most to us.

I wouldn't change anything about our life back then, but something was about to change soon, and it wasn't in our favor.

CHAPTER 11

Since the beginning of our homelessness, when we were about to get his room in a hostel in Stretham I didn't tell them about John's existence. I followed the advice of Jonas. Even when John joined us in February I didn't inform anybody from the hostel that he was living with us. I was afraid we would lose a place in this temporary accommodation. That was a big mistake.

As long as I was working everything was all right. But I wasn't working long time. That's when we started to have problems when I was unemployed. Our Housing Association wanted to know what income we were on. I didn't get any benefits. I didn't work. John was working, but he wasn't officially living with us. We didn't pay a lot for rent. It lasted a few months. I was trying to get some help in Citizen Advice Bureau, but I never got a good advice. I was looking for another job, but with no success either. I didn't have a clue how system was working with housing, and money. I didn't know who to turn to. Our situation became hopeless. In winter we got a letter from out Housing Association about eviction. We got a date when we should move out from that property. It was in a few weeks' time. We had only lived there for a little more than half of a year in this flat where we were so happy. It was a devastating news.

We had nowhere to go. Ewa had just started her school there. John's work was close too. Our happy life was shuttered in pieces. There was need for urgent emergency plan for our family. We couldn't afford to rent something similar to our flat privately. Prices in London are always expensive. The plan was like that: John was going to rent for himself a room somewhere, and we were going back to Poland for a few weeks with children until John was able to rent a flat for all of us again. That was the only idea we came up with. Of course we were going to my parents' house.

Last time I saw my parents in summer holidays when we visited them with children. A little more than a year ago my mother left me alone with children in England, because I had been turned down by an employer in Cornwall. I wasn't happy that she was leaving. Actually it was a little bit hurtful to me. I thought she wanted to help, but by the first obstacle on our way I was left alone with children. Maybe I shouldn't blame her. It had to be a little too much for her. She was in a strange country, she didn't speak English. To make matters worse her luggage was stolen in National Express bus on the way to Cornwall. She wasn't used to being dependent on anybody, but she was dependent on me because of language barrier. She is my mother, and I will always defend her no matter what she does. But feeling reveal the truth. Deep down inside me I knew she didn't care about us with kids at all. She was worried only about herself. There were many proves of this simple truth in my life.

I was born five years before my only brother. When he was born he quickly became my mother's favorite child. I don't know what was wrong with me. Maybe I was born in a wrong time? When I was young I was very often sent to my grandmother's place, which is 700 kilometers from home. Grandma, and auntie were taking care of me. My parents weren't even present when I was christened. My auntie organized my christening, and it took place in Church in Ostrowiec, where she lived. I didn't mind. I loved my grandma, and auntie. I always had a good time with them. We were playing cards, baking cakes, going shopping. In the summer we were going to the swimming-pool, which I liked the most. I don't know what my mother was doing when I was away.

On the other side my brother was always with my mother. She couldn't lose him of her sight. Maybe I was my father's favorite.

The special way my mother treated Thomas caused always problems between mother, and father. She was overprotective. She didn't pay no mind to father. To take a good care of Thomas was her only priority.

I wasn't short of anything in my childhood. I cannot complain about that. But money cannot buy everything.

Mother is like that: she doesn't like to waste time with people. She prefers to pay them, and to be left alone.

I don't want to judge her, but that's the way it is, and it has always been with everybody. Especially with me.

So far there were a lot of times when I needed financial support. I'm not proud of that. My parents always came to my rescue. I'm grateful for that to them. But sometimes you need to talk to your mother, to have shoulder to cry on, which I never have. She is, and she has always been busy. Too busy for me,

I'm always kidding myself: 'Yes she likes to talk to me, Yes she likes to know what is going on in my life, and how are the children'. I try to call her very often, but when I don't do that she doesn't complain.

It's like that because I don't have any friends, except from those on Face Book, who I write with. I don't meet anybody. I don't talk to people in the street. That's why I like to talk to my mother.

After all these years I should be used to that she doesn't like to talk to me. But I'm not. Every time it happens it hurts.

Maybe that's the character she has. She doesn't let people be close to her.

It was hard to announce to my parents our situation. They were happy for us that we had a flat, car, and John had a good job. I didn't want to involve them in another drama in our life. But we had nowhere else to go, I had to tell them, and ask for permission to do that. I was sure they would say 'yes'.

It was also hard to say 'good bye' to John. We had been reunited for a little more than a year, and then we had to be separated again.

Tough decision had to be made. You have to do what you can afford, and put feelings aside. This was the reality we had to face one more time.

I felt sorry for Ewa, because she had just started her new school a few months before. And then she was forced to leave it, which was heartbreaking to me. It's difficult to explain to little children like that what is going on. They don't understand many things. Even bigger children don't understand, because they don't want to. They live in their own childish world. They have different problems than adults connected with school, and their friends, and we have to respect that. That's why to take them away from their school so suddenly is a big shock to them, and shock is never good.

We had to make that journey to Poland again, and leave behind our English life for a few weeks. John took us to the bus stop in Central London. We said 'good bye' to each other. We didn't know when we will see each other again. Hopefully soon. Poland here we go!

Every move of mine was connected with lack of money. Not because I wanted to, but because I had to. That's terrible not to have a choice. Just to go with the flow of poverty leaving your husband behind not for the first time. That's the story of my life. I wish I could stay by my husband's side, but I cannot afford it. It kept happening to me many times in different countries. It was high time to put a stoppage to it. The only way to avoid situation like that is through work.

Somehow I didn't think about that back then. I didn't think that maybe I should get a job too to help the situation. I always knew that I had to take care of children. Nurseries, nannies were expensive, and we couldn't afford it, and job was hard to find for me. I didn't miss work at all. I was happy as a home maker. It suited me all these years.

We were welcome by my parents in Poland. We were back into our little one room in their big house. Even my brother had a much bigger room although he lived alone.

We couldn't feel so comfortable there. We were supposed to leave in a few weeks time.

You don't really know what your other half is doing when you don't see them. We trusted each other. But trust is on one side while on the other there are thousand of stupid thoughts inside your head. Especially when he doesn't pick up his phone. These thoughts are leading to one question: is he faithful to me? I should be more jealous when John had been to Jamaica, but I'm always jealous. At least we were on the same continent this time. I just like to know what he is up to every day.

I know he doesn't like to tell me that. In normal circumstances he usually doesn't tell me where he is going. I'm lucky when he tells me 'soon come' while leaving the house. Sometimes he is out long hours, and I never know where he is. Not to mention picking the phone by my husband. I'm lucky when he picks up his mobile when I'm calling him. Even for the safety reasons people should tell each other where they are going, but John is different. I'm used to that, but I don't like it.

I remember one Easter a few years ago John was in a bad mood. On Sunday morning he cooked dinner, and while I was with children in Church he left the house. Usually we celebrate Easter together., but this year was different. I was calling him like crazy, but there was no reply. I will never forget these two days. I was so worried about him. I think he finally picked up his phone on Monday evening. It was relief to me. John was all right. But Easter was spoilt that year.

Just like a lot of our birthdays, or Christmas days. He doesn't care. If John is not in a mood, he cannot pretend. That's why he lets us down on those special occasions from time to time, and nothing can be done about it. You cannot force people to do what they don't want to. As simple as that.

Maybe he feels bad too about all those spoilt celebrations in our life. Maybe he would like to be different.

People don't change. He will probably do it again, and I'm not looking forward to it. Thankfully I have my children to celebrate with me special days. They never let me down.

We spent in Poland six weeks only, so that's not long. It was winter time, so there was not much to do. I was on the phone with John every day to make sure he was doing everything in his power to bring us back to England. I missed him so much. I should have been used to that longing, but it never comes easy. He missed us too. He was living in a room somewhere far from his work. Work was going well. He didn't complain. That was only positive thing in this whole situation.

When you live on your own, and suddenly you are forced to live with your parents again that's not a nice feeling. They were used to being on their own, and I had been independent before. Besides we'd just visited them a few months before in the summer with children. That should be enough. But we had to pay them visit in winter, which was shameful. They were helping us during that difficult time, but I don't really know what they were thinking about us. Probably all the bad things. As usual. But that's not my problem. I had to protect my children. That's why we were there.

Life can make surprising turns sometimes, and nothing cannot be done to change it. We have to accept it whenever we like it, or not. You just have to know where you belong, and what is important, and build your life around it.

Nothing bad happened to anyone. We all needed to have a little patience, and have faith that soon things will be back to normal. I am never short of faith. I'm a believer. I believe in brighter future to come. Always. In every situation I am in. It helps me a lot. Some people may feel sorry for me, but there is no need for that. I believe that this is my way, and I have to follow it. Like a destiny, which has to be fulfilled.

Everybody wants only good things happen to them. Of course. That's natural. But just like we welcome them we should welcome the bad ones too. We can treat them like a lesson to learn. The quicker we learn, the quicker we will be back to normal. Afterwards we will be able to appreciate positive aspects of our life.

People might say that it's all my fault. That I put us in this crisis. I don't think it's true. In some situations there is no one to blame. It's just like that. Danger appear out of nowhere to attack people.

One Christmas I made a terrible mistake. On Christmas day I got a call from my mother. She wanted us with children to visit them. We were living back then with John in a building in town center. I said 'no' to her. We went with children to Church. My parents came after church service, and they insisted for us to visit them. So we went, while John was alone at home on Christmas day. We spent there a few hours. When we finally returned home John was furious. I didn't expect that. Jamaican father, and Polish mother of two cannot sit together by Christmas tree under one roof, can they? No! Because parents didn't like that.

To be honest John from the very first day we met in this beautiful park in Ouchy told me about this special love he had for his grandparents. His mother carried him as a baby to their house in Caledonia(St. Ann).There were three people in this house back then including his beloved uncle. Church was very close to that house in the mountains.

Every Sunday they were in Church. John attended Sunday school before each mass. His grandfather was a farmer. They have animals, and crops on the farm. In the spare time he was a preacher.

John slept in one bed with his uncle. He kept repeating to me this story over, and over again how his uncle took him to local pub one evening to drink rum, and he gave John some. As far as I know he was being single all his life helping his parents with animals, and plants. John was helping him as a little kid. They were going to the forest together with a donkey to get wood for cooking, and something to eat. They often show Blue Mountains in those shows about Jamaica. I have never been there, and neither was John (it's the hottest place on that small island).

I simply hate the heat. Even in Swinoujscie, whare I was brought up, I didn't like it in the summer. Every June the weather is slowly changing. You go to school in the morning. It's quite nice. But just after you come back home, eat something, and that's it. You just have to go to your room to lay down, and basically do nothing.

At the end of this month we had summer holidays, so the whole of July I was going to the beech. As a kid I was going with my parents. A little later with my best friend from the play ground Anka, and Agnieszka from primary school,as a teenager with boys on the bikes in the days. I had friends back then. Now I don't, which is a shame. Everybody is on Face Book. I like Face Book, because I like to write. I don't use any video calls with anybody. I just don't feel comfortable to do that.

When I was in High School there was DOS as operating system., not WINDOWS yet. I know that internet is great, but I'm not in love with it yet.

It's helping a lot of people, but behind those screens there are real people working to make it run. Some people might forget about it.

My parents don't use touch screen technology. I cannot add my mother on Face Book. She cannot be my 'friend' on Face Book. It's not good. I could send her more pictures, and we could write to each other.

My cousin Ewa is on FB, and we write everything to each other. It's been almost five years now our Face Book friendship. I had an occasion to meet her, and her husband when we were last time visiting my parents in Poland. They came to Swinoujscie to visit my parents for a few days. It was weird at first to face her, because I had been writing to her everything about my life. It's still going on. She is a great help to me, clever with a good heart. I can always count on her. I hope we will meet again soon.

I love my mother, but she doesn't even like to talk to me on the phone. I'm sure of that. Children always laugh at me that I call, and later on get mad at her. I'll never stop calling her. She brought me up. She was encouraging me to make my dreams come true. She was telling me compliments. She should get an award for that. Not every mother is like that. Father spent most of his time at work abroad as a seaman. He didn't help her to bring us with my brother up. Everything was on mother's head.

I cannot complain about my childhood. I learnt a lot at schools I was going to. I was always a good student, and books meant everything to me. Father was always trying to put me in a right direction with my education, and my career. Not every parents do that.

I grew up in communist times. Eastern Europe was separated from the Western Europe by the wall in Berlin, a capital of Germany. Communism collapsed in 1981 thanks to Pope John the Second, and electrician from shipyard in Polish city Gdansk Lech Walesa. He became the first president in democratic Poland.

I was born in 1976. Five years of my life I spent in those times. We lived in a studio flat. In those times everybody should be equal, and have equal opportunities. It was hard to get anything in the shops. Shelves were basically empty. If there was something on the shelves there were long queues. That was our reality back then.

My father was once arrested, because Police found bananas in our flat. They were accusing him of selling illegal products from abroad.

Luckily we always had a car so we could go to different nearby towns to search for things in shops like meat, eggs, clothes. I don't know a lot about politics, but I can imagine life like that had to be hard for everybody.

Now it's simple. You have got the money, you can buy, and do everything you want.

But before although you had money, you couldn't find things you needed.

On the east from Poland there used to be Russia, our big brother. This country was feeding, and clothing us. Russians were even building high buildings with a lot of flats in it.

Communist system was created by Karl Marx German philosopher in 19th century. Europe was divided after the second world war. Eastern side was communist, and western democratic. The idea of communism was good, but it didn't work in real life. People like to be free, and have access to everything. Fortunately my country is not communist any more. World is changing around us, and we even don't see that. Small changes are better than big ones. Big ones can shock people, and make them feel bad.

CHAPTER 12

I know what I like, but I didn't like the place John'd arranged for us before we came back from Poland with children.

He picked us up from the Standstead Airport by taxi, because this time we took a plane. We spent around six weeks in Poland by this occasion, so it's not so long.

Our room was in a basement. We had to share a bathroom with other family, who lived in the next room. Children had their bunk bed. We were sleeping on a mattress on the floor. There also was cooker inside that room.

The people next door were fighting all the time. They had one child.

I hated living in that basement. I hated it!

Thankfully John quickly found a different place for us to live. I was so happy about that.

To share a bathroom with anybody is terrible. I had had so many problems with that in the past.

First time it happened in Polish city called Lodz. My grandfather lived there, and that's where my father was brought up.

After I had finished High School I went to Lodz to study building in University. My grandfather rented me a room. I was sharing kitchen, and bathroom with woman called Basia. I had a boyfriend back then, and one evening I was expecting to see him. He was going to visit me. From Swinoujscie to Lodz is far (around 700 km). I was waiting, and waiting for him, but he was nowhere to be seen. Basia told me to clean the toilet, which we were sharing in that house. I couldn't even clean toilet, because my mother had never taught me to do that. We had an argument with Basia over this dirty toilet. My boyfriend still wasn't coming. I had enough. I left the house in dress only bare feet although it was winter. I was running through the streets of Lodz. I was out of my mind. I reached my grandfather's house, but he didn't open the door, because it was late. Ambulance took me to the hospital. I guess neighbors called the ambulance.

That was the first time I was mentally sick.

The other incident with toilet occurred also in Lodz.

My grandfather died in 2006, and his will was to give me his house.

We went to live in this house in 2008 with John, and kids. There are two parts in this house. Some people were loving in one part, and we were living in another. There was only one toilet there to share again.

Although it was my grandfather's house woman next door told me that we should clean the bathroom in turns. One week she was going to do that, and the other one me.

When my turn came I did my best. But it wasn't good enough. I was told that I didn't do the tails on the wall. I never do the tails even now. I had enough of these commands from a stranger. I did my best, as I said. It was happening in the morning. There was an argument between me and she. In the afternoon my husband came back from work. He wanted to use toilet, but the door to the toilet was closed. People, who we were living with under one roof closed the toilet, because I didn't clean it properly. John confronted them, and there was a big fight between three of them John, man, and a woman. I didn't take part in that fight. I was just watching. It happened in their part of the house. A few hours later we heard a knock on our door. It was this trouble maker with his friends, and dangerous dog on leash to worn us that he was not alone. I was so scared of this dog. John was shocked. In my grandfather's house such a disrespectful thing happened to us.

I made again bad move, like in Switzerland, and came back to live in my parents' house without John. This situation was too much to bear. John stayed alone in Lodz.

I was 'safe' in my parents' house. I was waiting, and wondering what move my husband make? I didn't know what is going on, and what to do. It felt like it was a complete disaster. I didn't like to be without John, and especially I didn't like to live with my parents again. When I think about it things can go wrong over everything. Even dirty toilet can be a reason, which is stupid. Some things are more important than others.

After a few weeks living in that basement John found us a proper flat to rent. It was situated on the first floor in a quiet area near Crystal Palace Stadium. There was nice park very close to our flat. I found new school for children. It wasn't so close to that school from home. I'm not complaining. I like to walk. John had got a job a few weeks before we rented a flat. We could have fresh start together as a family. I like to have some comfort in life. It makes me feel good. I also want the best for my children, and John. I don't want us to suffer.

Life was good again. I was happy. Even there was nearby Polish Catholic Church. Some Sundays I used to take children there.

That's what probably miss the most in UK- Polish Catholic Church. There is one in Birmingham, but I have never been there yet. There is Polish community around that Church. People meet up, and there are many different events in that place. I should go to this St. Michael's Church one Sunday.

In my Church here there is no confession very often. In Poland priests are almost always doing confession during the mass.

Fortunately I have already learnt most prayers in English which we say on mass gatherings.

Ewa, and Pawel took this sacrament of Holly Communion here in UK. Now I will have to christen Emilia, because soon she will have to prepare for taking her Holly Communion too. First she has to be christen.

The problem with christening Emilia is that we don't have anybody for her to be her God parents. I should christen her in Poland.

Ewa was christened when she was one year old, Pawel at the age of three months. Emilia still not christened although she is four.

My character is like that. I don't like strange people to be in my house. It makes me nervous, and uncomfortable. I am not the one to throw parties. I don't like to go to parties either. I'm just not this type of person.

John came from Lodz to Swinoujscie to see us with children. I didn't expect that. He stayed in a nearby hotel.

It was good to see him. It's always good to see John. And I forgave him although there was nothing to forgive. He didn't do nothing wrong. He told me he was still working in Lodz after we had left.

How do we always do that? Why we forgive each other? Through sex of course. We need each other. Chemistry is there always. This spark when John first touched me in his sister's house in my waist will be probably with me forever. That's what keeps our relationship alive.

Every summer when we go to Poland for holidays I miss him a lot. We usually spend six weeks there.

Two times John was with us in Swinoujscie. He had a good time. I was happy that John had occasions to meet my parents. They were nice to him.

I think they regret the way had treated him before. But harm was done. It was too late to play happy family.

My parents has a big house. My brother lives with them. He's just got married for the second time, and they are expecting a child.

Parents are afraid about who would take care of them in the future. When they would be too old to do that themselves. So far so good. They have each other, and Thomas. They have difficulties with walking. My mother uses walking stick. Father a few years ago underwent knee replacement surgery.

Father always complains about his health (he also has asthma from the longest time), but mother doesn't. She even doesn't go to see a doctor. She still works part-time in her herbal shop.

So many times I had this idea to go to work in her shop., but I love England. Besides my mother wouldn't want me to leave children behind with John.

England is the place to be for me, and for my family. John is complaining from time to time, but he just wants to get an attention. Deep down inside he knows it too. Everyone is respected here, and has a chance to live decent live.

I knew that the first time I came here. I saw children live stress-free live. Now I know that not only children experience that. As long as you have some job you are all right. British people are nice. If you are in need, there is help. We try every day with John to' make it happen' for the sake of our children.

The worse is when we disagree about something, and when it happens very often. Shame on us. I always want my plans to be put in action. John is not having it most of times. He likes to do it his way, and in his time. It's difficult to deal with him. He would never say 'yes', let's do it darling. Basically he is against everything I want to do with him.

When he was younger in his 30ties he wasn't like that. He enjoyed work, and he was nicer to me. With time you lose your drive. It's harder, because you have less strength.

I don't know too much about work. Most of time I worked in Poland, not in England, where most of time I spent taking care of children, and house.

Most people are at work. Men, women. But I am not.

My cousin Ewa from Poland, who is ten years older than me wrote to me once on Face Book that she was already tired of working (she works as a shop assistant in corner shop). She used to take care of her younger siblings (there were eight of them altogether). Her parents were alcoholics.

To get money as a kid she used to pick up fruits, and sell them in the market.

The same John. He is the oldest from his siblings. His auntie, who was a teacher, always asked him to take care of her children. His mother always treated him worse than the rest of his brothers, and sisters, but he had to help her with everything. She was selling goods in the market.

That's why John is not like me, and he will never be. But I love him to bits.

Just after finishing secondary school he started to work as a welder to have his own money. He had no other choice. Now after all these years of work he must be tired like my cousin Ewa. My type of work is easier than his. I always admire him. I know he is a good worker. Always on time, full of respect towards his colleagues.

Unlike me, who loses one job after another. Somehow managers are not impressed by my attitude towards work. Maybe, just maybe I haven't find my destiny yet. I have to look for it, and never give up.

My disadvantage is my illness. It's always stopping us in our way. Situations keep repeating themselves. Most of the time John loses his job, because I get sick. Employers are not interested in those dramas in our life. They want you at work, and not at home taking care of sick wife.

Every month it was a struggle to pay rent for this flat near Crystal Palace Studium. John was working on sides in different nearby places. I wasn't working all this time. We were going with children to this park close to our house. They learnt to ride their bikes without stabilizers. We were so proud of them with John. We were also going to for walks to various places, sometimes even to Central London by car, or by bus to visit West Minster, parliament of Great Britain. It wasn't far from where we lived.

I don't know why, but somehow we didn't know back then that London is the place to be. People from all over the world want to come here to work, or study. They pay more in London for work than anywhere else. There are top

Universities in London. Many theatres, museums, art galleries, opera, night clubs, huge shopping centers. There are almost endless possibilities for Londoners. It's easy to commute, because there are a lot of buses, and of course underground. We didn't know how good for us was being there.

Now when we go to London we always have to go to Oxford Street, the best street to do shopping. We go there from time to time. John from time to time still mention London. He regrets that we left. It was too expensive for us to live there. Rent is expensive there, and shops are not cheap either. We used to pay much more for rent in London than here. And it was 15 years ago.

I remember I always wanted to go to some premiers of films to see some famous actors, and actresses. But I never went. It was just within my hands reach, but it didn't happen.

Now I want to go to Warsaw, capital of Poland to see some of my adored by me Polish celebrities. And I want to go to visit Ewa, and the rest of my family from the south of Poland.

I would like to be rich, and famous. Maybe in that position I could make the difference, and help people less fortunate than me. I want to be good. So far I'm living for myself, and my family only. John says that we all are selfish with children. I want to change that. To do that I must set an example for my children first. How to be good? Is it easy, or difficult?

We are used to not share anything with children. Everybody has to have their own. John shares. The answer to these questions are in Holy Bible, how to be good. God is good. We must just follow in his footsteps.

I wish somebody would recognize me for being good.

We bought some furniture to live comfortable like sofa, bed for us with John, and bunk bed for the kids. They shared a room. We were sleeping in living-room with John.

I like where we live now. Nothing wrong with our place. We rent from Housing Association in Darlaston three bedroom house with a garden. John applied for us, and after a few months we got it.

There is park close to the house, supermarket Asda, Catholic Church, and library. It's not far to the big town Walsall. By bus it takes 15-20 minutes to get there. Birmingham is not far either, but we don't go there very often.

I wish we could go to all places in UK. The most intriguing place to me seems to be Scotland. My dream is to go to Edinburgh. And it will come true sooner rather than later. I just have to work towards it.

We were living in this flat near Crystal Palace stadium a few months only.

One day in autumn I got sick again. My mental health problems came back. John didn't know how to handle it. I was talking nonsense, and my behavior was not normal (I just wasn't myself). He took me to the hospital to A&E. Children were with us of course.

When you have mental health illness it's not like any other one. It's not like a headache, or stomachache. You look all right like nothing is wrong with you, but deep down inside you know the difference. You are not in a control of the situation. You cannot sleep, eat, you are being paranoid. Of course you don't even realize that you are sick, and refuse to take any medication. You can be violent too towards other people.

Hospital we went to sent us to another hospital, because they didn't know how to help me.

It was such a stressful situation. From the other hospital ambulance took me, because I was out of control. John followed ambulance with children by car to see where they were taking me.

Thankfully I was allowed to stay in this specialist hospital. They sectioned me for three days. After that period of time they had put me on medication for mental health illness, and I was free to go with prescription for them. I was going to take them at home.

John was with kids at home. They visited me while I was still in that hospital. In London, just like here in Black Country we had nobody to help us in situations like that. No help whatsoever.

My husband lost his job, because of time off he had taken to take care of children, and me during that time. He didn't have a contract then. He was just temporary worker from work agency.

It was devastated for us. We didn't have any money coming into our bank account any more. Nothing at all. And no help from anybody. No benefits. Of course no savings. I even couldn't afford to buy my prescription from pharmacy.

Just after I had left the hospital home treatment team came to visit me a few times. They knew the situation we were in. They felt sorry for us. One day even they brought us some grocery shopping.

The reason why we couldn't get any benefits was because John didn't have a permit from Home Office. His visa had expired a long time ago.

Somehow John found another job quickly, but it wasn't as good as the previous one. They didn't pay the same amount of money. They were paying less. Every month we could afford to pay rent, but not all of it. Areas were increasing, and increasing. We owed our landlord a lot of money after a few months like that. We didn't pay our gas, and electricity bills. I was all the time looking through the window, waiting for gas, and electricity companies vans to cut the supply of gas, and electricity off (fortunately they never came).

To live like that on the edge is terrible. Everybody is doing what they can, but it's not good enough. It wasn't our first year in England. It was our fourth year, so we should have been settled.

My parents were sending me money occasionally to help us a little bit. It always felt, and it still feels (because they still are doing it) like somebody believes in you, like somebody is giving you a chance.

My mother would like me to always have money to spend. I admire her a lot, and so does John. Children loves her, even Emilia, who cannot speak Polish tells her through the phone that she loves her.

She is independent, running her own business. She has been doing that for more than twenty years. John would like me to be like she, but I'm interested in other things.

My cousin Ewa works in corner shop in Poland. When I wanted to go to work in my mother's shop I asked Ewa what she thinks about it. She wrote to me back that you have to work in shop from Monday to Saturday like for example she. I have artistic character, and I like to do things in my own time only. Even housework I do when I want to, not when I have to. only

From my experience with working with people I had bad memories, because I cannot stand up for myself. My colleagues only used to push me around. I didn't like it, but I wouldn't say a word. I just take it as it is.

It's hard to work for me. Everybody from my family should be used to that by now. I take light things too hard, too personal. What would be nothing to somebody else is a big problem to me. I don't like to ask for help if I cannot do it myself.

When John is out of work we have to rely on benefits. John always prefers to work. Sometimes it's not my illness is stopping him from work. He has also health issues himself. He likes to make things. It makes him happy. He has pride in what he is doing. That's good. Many people around us were telling him to change profession, but he doesn't want to hear that.

Sometimes he has problem with his back, sometimes with his heart. He is on medication for coronary heart disease, and heart blood pressure.

It's very good that there is this benefit system here. I don't know what would we without it? I hadn't known about those possibilities when I was leaving Poland for England. Even here it took us four years to find out about benefits like Child Benefits, Child Tax Credit, Housing Benefits. Before we had rented privately.

We are safe here. We have to pay rent, but when John doesn't have a job it's paid through benefits.

When we were living in London we couldn't claim any benefits, because James didn't have a permit. He couldn't even get a visa to go to Poland, because of that.

All money we had back then was from John's earnings. So no work, no money.

Things keep repeating to people like us over, and over again. There is no way to stop that circle. I wish it was different, but it's not.

John would like to open his own business. He thinks that would save us from financial difficulties. But you need some money to start, which we don't have.

Money, money, money, money. That's our main topic with Jonh every day. To pay this, to pay that, and not much left till the next payday. That's the reality we face most of the time. I wish it would end one day, but it looks like it's never-ending.

Sometimes I think it's my fault, that I don't get enough, and always want more. One thing leads to another. I want for myself, and for my kids, more, and more. I cannot stop. Of course John doesn't allow me to do that. He controls most of our money.

Most of the days I'm without money at all. That's my punishment for not keeping money.

What is important to me that somehow we have managed to stay with my husband for such a long time against all adds. Many unpleasant things happened to him since we are together. Very many. Not only rejection from my family. In the biggest troubles he was always crossing the borders. Always innocent, but often something went wrong. That's the best way to describe my John.

First time since I know him he was stopped on the boarder with between Poland, and Germany while going to visit me, and my family in Poland. He was the only black man on the bus. But they let him go.

Next time he had some problems, because he came to Poland with invalid passport. He was stopped by boarder control in Germany while leaving Poland. John was travelling by bus again coming back to England. Bus left without him. Father had to buy him plane ticket to Manchester.

Even bad thing happened to us when we were travelling together, just me, and him to Walsall. By bus again. In Calais English immigration stopped us. Bus left without us. As soon as they let us through we took a ferry to Dover, and came to Birmingham by National Express bus. Fortunately we didn't have to pay for the ferry, and that bus, but we were late. Our journey took longer that we had expected.

The worse for sure was for John when Polish Boarder Control deported him to Jamaica. Before he had been kept in Deportation Center in Szczecin, which was basically like prison for a few weeks.

CHAPTER 13

Life becomes easier when children start to go to school. Most of mums love their kids, but they need a break from taking care of them. With Ewa, and Pawel I always had this advantage that they could always play together, because they were similar age (Pawel had been born 1.5 years after Ewa).

While John was burning steel at work I was with them. Now I have got this feeling that I didn't appreciate what my husband was doing for us every day. It seemed ordinary to me. Not a big deal. So many years I wasn't working, and through all these years it wasn't a problem to John. Taking care of children, and housework is a kind of work too, but in England a lot of women work, while they have children.

I am old-fashioned. Women make a lot of movements like feminism. They protest, they want the same pay as men when they do the same job. Women work as drivers, firefighters, Police officers, astronauts. No limits for women now.

But for somebody like me there are only limits. No work, no money, no being able to drive. I just don't like to take those responsibilities on my back. That's the way I am, and I cannot change for anybody, because adults don't change. Character is in our genes. And no matter how hard we try we cannot change it.

Basically all I have my husband bought me.

One day when we were still leaving in flat near Crystal Palace Stadium Jonh had promised our landlord certain sum of money towards the rent into landlord's bank account. John gave me the money. I was the one to go to the bank to do that. I didn't pay the whole amount to his account. I spent a few pounds out of this money to pay for pictures in children's school. I thought it wouldn't make any difference to our landlord.

But it made a huge difference. A few days later we got a notice.

Again we were about to lose another flat. What to do? We were in the same position as before not that long ago. In 2006 we had lost council flat in Sydenham. This time it was private landlord. No matter what kind of accommodation we were in, we were losing them one after another. Our flat had been rented unfurnished, so we had to buy our own furniture. When we were living this flat, we left all our furniture. John had spent so much money on them for nothing. His hard work for nothing.

We were devastated with John. Children were forced to leave their school. It's hard to think about it. Broken life. You are happy somewhere, and you cannot stay there. Things like that you see on television, but if it happens to you something is wrong. Nobody want their life to be a horror story.

London is expensive. John managed to rent for himself room somewhere far from his work. And I took children to Poland to stay in my parents' house. Good thing that parents welcome us always with opened arms. I don't know what they thought about me, but I just needed roof over our heads for some time.

It was so sad to say good bye to John. We didn't know when we would see each other again.

This time I had to go to work, and children went to school in Poland. I quickly got a job in a nearby pharmacy in small shopping center. It was a good job. I could pay rent to my father.

Of course parents were helping me with everything as much as they could. But I missed John, and our life in UK. My place was by his side. I couldn't fight this feeling. I was just waiting for him to give us 'ok' to come back to London.

I liked my work in this pharmacy. My boss was younger than me. He introduced me to internet. Before I hadn't been interested in using internet at all. The most interesting portal he showed me was Pudelek. It's a gossip website about life of Polish, and other celebrities. I read it still every day. It's interesting to me. I am into gossip stories. That's the only contact I have got to know what is going on in Poland (except talking to my parents).

I always prefer to talk to people face to face. I even don't like to talk over the phone.

Technology was forced into people whenever they wanted too, or not. I cannot keep up with it. Modern world. Nobody asked us if we wanted to live in it, or not. Those endless possibilities are not for somebody like me. All I like is my pen, and paper, and my music. That's my technology. And of course books, and magazines are important to me.

I'm interested in royal family. They don't have royal family in Poland. My favorite royals are Prince William, and Kate Middleton with their three children: George, Charlotte and Louise. I also like Prince Charles, and Camilla. And of course Her Majesty the Queen.

William's brother is called Harry. At the beginning of this year he, and his wife decided to simply leave royal family, and move out of UK. I know I don't even know them, and probably I will never get to know them, but I was so mad with them. Everybody from my family was laughing at me, but I couldn't forgive this royal couple. People used to love them, and they gave this love away. I couldn't believe that. I was shocked. There are not so many princes, and princesses in this world.

Harry's wife is called Meghan, and she is an American actress. They got married three years together, and they have one son together called Archie.

People from royal family have a lot of duties. We have Prime Minister, and Queen. Queen is not involved in politics.

They travel a lot to represent our country. People from abroad come to visit them.

What I like about all of them is that they set an example how people should live. Ordinary people can relate to them.

Queen is over ninety years old, and her husband will be a hundred soon. She will keep the crown till the end of her life. That's how much she loves what she is doing. She is very far from her husband most of the time, because he had stepped down from royal duties a couple of years ago due to his old age. He spends most of his time in Sandringham, which is in Scotland. They had just celebrated their 73rd wedding anniversary.

John also likes royal family. Especially he respects those members who served in an Army like Harry.

Jamaica had been British colony before 1962. A lot of Jamaicans had come to fight on the front line for Britain in the World War Two. Three years after people from this nation came to rebuild our country after this war. Between 1948 and 1970 nearly half a million people moved from the Caribbean to Britain to work here. Some of them traveled from Jamaica, and other Caribbean countries by ship called 'Windrush'.

People from those counties are called now 'Windrush Generation', because of the name of that ship. I saw video on television, when they were coming by ship in the news. Recently families of people from these Caribbean countries were fighting with government here for their rights. I think some of them couldn't stay in UK, because they couldn't get proper documents.

Black people not only come from Africa. Before I had met John I wasn't interested in history of black people. I only admired black singers like Usher, Puff Daddy, Whitney Huston. My favorite singer Mariah Carey collaborated with many black musician including Jay Z. I also liked Beyonce, and Rihanna.

When I met John I thought my life would be like in a music videos with my black man.

But it wasn't.

Slavery times are over. Britain is no longer an Empire, as it had been before. But John every time he gets a job he says he gets a worse treatment than the white workers, only because a colour of his skin. I think he is a little too sensitive, but only he knows how he feels. Once he even made a complaint to his manager about it. There had been an investigation, but no one was rebuked. Instead of being proud of who he is he feels worse than the others. I'm sorry for him. Maybe one day he will feel differently. I hope so.

Queen established Common Wealth 11th of December 1931. Jamaica, and many other countries all over the world owned by British Empire got a kind of freedom. People from those countries were still owned by Britain, but they could set up their own rules, and regulations.

Many of them fought for independence, and so did Jamaica.

I am not a specialist from Jamaican history, but my husband says that it was unfair what British people were doing in previous centuries to black people. Also other nations were conquered by Great Britain from different continents like Africa, or Asia. These were terrible times. They had conquered these continents, and later they made colonies out of them. They did it just to get rich, but they didn't care about people.

Technology was on their side. Ships, weapons, later on trains, cars and phones.

No matter if you are black, Asian, or mixed race you should get the same treatment all over the world. The reason why black people turned to crime more often than white ones is because of this injustice. They don't have equal opportunities to get a job. Police stop them more often than the white ones. You look around and see that white people get good jobs, and you have less chances than them you are sad. Sometimes even you might get mad, and do something stupid, which you would later regret.

When you are struggling in foreign country you might think that's it would be better to come back to your country. At least your own people respect you.

When you come for example to UK to work English people maybe think badly about your country. That is poor, and no good. It's not always is the case. Jamaica is a poor country, but Poland is not. Polish people get help from the government just like here, and work is easy to find.

I had came here to be with John. Later on I fell in love with this country. I would never want to go back to Poland to live. I haven't visited many places in Great Britain, but I'm planning to do so pretty soon. The most intriguing place for me is Scotland. But it's far from where we live. One day we will get there at the end. Edinburgh looks in the pictures magical. It remands me of Prague.

Not to mention coast line we have. We have already been to Blackpool when I was pregnant with Emilia. After she had been born we visited Minehead, and Brighton. I was a little afraid of these tides, because I don't know anything about them. My father's friend died because of tides. He was taking picture at sea. Tide had came, and he drowned.

I love Blackpool, because of these lights in the evening, light up carriages with horses, rocks to eat. The atmosphere is amazing there. We went to Blackpool at the end of October. People are relaxed, not always on their phones.

To Minhead we went, because Pawel's football team were taking part in tournament. We stayed in Butlins for two for nights. I think it was bank holiday weekend. Pawel had a good time with his mates. There was swimming-pool there, and even fun fair. I the most like about our stay there the concert. The singer was singing Jessy J songs. We like Jessy J with Ewa.

I booked Premier Inn hotel in Brighton for us the year when I was working. Ewa is making vlogs, and posts them on YouTube. She desperately wanted to go to Brighton, because her favorite vloggers Alfie Deyes, and Zoe Sugg live in Brighton. So we went to Brighton. I cannot tell you what Brighton is like, because I felt bad there. Again side effects of aripiprazole (tablets I was taking for my bipolar disorder) affected me. I had already started to feel bad on the way to Brighton, in the car. I remember when we were going to use the toilet with John in McDonald's in Brighton I was asking him to wait for me, because I wouldn't be able to come back to the car on my own. When we were reaching our hotel I was hoping that I would be able to check in. My eyes didn't work properly when I was experiencing these side effects. My psychiatrist told me that it happens very rarely. It was easy to check in. As soon as I had arrived to our hotel room, I went to bed. John took children out. I couldn't go nowhere. Fortunately when they had came back I was normal again. We talked almost the whole night. Next day it was raining. We went to see the beach. First time I was on the beach with only stones. I took one stone as a souvenir. Emilia was little then. She was still in the pram. John didn't want her to get sick. We had eaten in McDonald's, and because of bad weather we headed straight back home. It was around midday. I was very disappointed.

During this year when I was working in pharmacy we also went for a day to Stratford-upon-Avon. I think it was in May. I'm interested in writing, so I wanted to see Shakespeare's house. Of course all of us couldn't sightsee his house, because of horrendous prices of tickets. We were lucky with Ewa to go there. It was very interesting to me. We even saw actors performing one of his play in the garden. I bought 'Hamlet' book in souvenir shop. I was so happy about that. John found some park for Emilia to play on the playground when we were with Ewa in this museum.

These are the places we never come back too. But there are some places nearby which we like, and go there from time to time.

My definitely favorite one from those places is Lichfield. In Lichfield there is medieval English cathedral with three spires. There is also nice playground for Emilia to play, and a big pound.

For shopping the best place to go is Birmingham. There is shopping center called Bull Ring. Very big one. Shops we go to there are Sports. Direct, Hmv, Hms, Primark, VictoriaSecrets, JD, Claire's, Disney, and Entertainer. In front of this shopping center there is a sculpture of brown bull.It's a good place to meet up with somebody.

I have already mentioned our love of London. Approximately we are there once a year. Before we had always been going for one day only. But the last two times we stayed one night in a hotel.

I love travelling. It can be a big adventure. I like to spend nights in hotels. My favorite one is Premier Inn.

In 2020 we stayed in different hotel in London. I was so disappointed. Our hotel was small, and our room was in a basement. Besides there was no hot water to have a shower. It was situated in Chelsea. But still we had a good time. Hotel was situated near Westfield shopping center. Pawel bought for himself suit to Sixth Form in shop called Next. Ewa got a few pieces of clothes in Hms Emilia chose Anna dolly from Frozen, which was singing in Disney. Me pink hoodie, and earrings in Hms. In the evening I took Ewa, and Pawel for a long walk to Kensington Palace, while Emilia stayed with John (she doesn't like to walk too much).

Trips to London by car are expensive, because after you come back you have to pay a lot for a lot altogether for Congestion Charge Zone in city center, Ultra Low Emission Zone, and Low Emission Zone. Emission Zones depends on what car you drive.

Soon Pawel will become driver, and I cannot wait. Hopefully he will be taking me places. All of us. He cannot wait for this moment either. John explains to him that he should rather concentrated on learning, and not thinking about driving. I want him to drive for selfish reason to have another driver in the house.

Sometimes it's so hard to drag John out of the house. Everybody is ready to go, and we are waiting for him to get out of bed, and take a shower. That's why I like to have some appointments to go to, so I know that John will take me there for sure.

My mother likes to go places too with my father. I must have taken this habit from her.

When we are all together in our new car I feel that we can conquer the world. The best moments of my life.

I have recently managed to get a big, new, family car on hire purchase. I'm happy to have it. It's much different than the one we had had before with sat-nav, seven seats, and dark windows at the back. I chose it. We can travel now long distances in UK, and through Europe. It was John's dream to drive car like that. His dream came true.

He never show happiness, and he doesn't like when I am too happy about something. Maybe it's childish, but I can be happy about small things. I am not like John. At least I have children to share my happiness with.

It's so good to have children. You know you won't be alone till the end of your life (in most cases it's like that). They bring joy to your life, but also worry. Ewa, and Pawel are crossing the threshold of adulthood. I hope we will always be close as we are now. I will do everything in my power to protect them. So far so good. They are good kids staying out of troubles.

Emilia will always be our baby girl. She will turn five next week. We had a bond with her with Ewa, and Pawel. We are close. But she doesn't listen. She likes to have her own way. We have to be strict with John with her. Otherwise we would have to listen to her. She doesn't know yet what is right, and what is wrong. John, and I want the best for her. Just like most parents.

I love her to bits. Every evening we talk in bed about different things. She is so clever. These are precious moments we share together.

I'm so happy when people are nice to her. We don't have any family here (except two John's brothers in London who we never see, and Patricia - John's cousin). Emila have already been to Poland to visit grandparents twice. When I was pregnant with Emilia my mother wasn't so sure that it was a good idea to have another baby. She was hoping for me to take over her shop after her in Poland.

I would never move out from England to Poland. My place is here, and the best chances for all of us. Only I cannot take advantage of them, because of my illness. I will be on medication until the end of my life. Some illnesses never end. The same situation is, and will be with Ewa. It's sad, but true. That's why I don't advice Ewa to go to work yet. She would like to work at weekends when there is no College. My opinion is to wait with that until she finishes College. I just don't want her to go through what I had been through with my jobs. She deserves better. Ewa is educated in Britain, and she should get a good job. The same Pawel. Recently my son has told me that he would like to become a truck driver. I was disappointed. I hope he will go to study at the University. He is a very good student. There are many truck drivers. I just don't want him to waste his talent, which he definitely has. It's his life, and I want the best for him. He is too young to know which path to choose. I am trying to help him to decide. Time is running quickly. Soon it will be time to make crucial decision. It's still one and a half years ago.

I'm so happy that Ewa, and Pawel stay at home most of the time. It means they like to live with us with John. They don't need to go out. They are close to me, and my husband, and that's our success. I also enjoy their company. It means I'm a good mum. I somehow managed to protect them. Life wasn't easy for Ewa, and Pawel where they were little, but nothing bad has happened to them.

Emilia has much better childhood then them. She is the lucky one. My little daughter is safe. I didn't have to drag her behind me to Poland two times atter getting notice letters in Britain.

Children like routine, stability, which I couldn't give to my two eldest children. Through first years of their life they life was chaotic. Travelling between England, and Poland, changing schools. I don't like changes, but life in those times were changing all the time around us. It's not my fault.

I'm in the good place now. Very good. It doesn't mean it will always be like that. The most important for me is to stay with John till the end our out life. He is my rock. I cannot imagine my life without him. Soon we will be celebrating our 17th wedding anniversary.

John doesn't like to celebrate anything. One day he said to my mother that when he has roof over his head, and food on the table it's holiday for him. Every day given us by God is special.

He says that all holidays are commercial. People make money out of it.

I love to celebrate. There is always something to wait for.

At the beginning of each year there is New Year's Day. I like New Year's day. It's a chance for me to start all over again. I don't make New Year's resolutions. I wake up this day only to see that everything is exactly the same.

14th of February we celebrate Valentine's day. I like it too. I always expect John to give me a nice present, while I am giving to him a card only, because I never have money for anything else. John never disappoints me. I always get something like a pretty robe, or flowers. Sometimes he gives me money to buy something myself. I'm childish. One year I bought for myself giant teddy bear with red flower in his paws.

At the beginning of March Emilia was born. My mother always sends me money for all our birthdays, so we always can buy nice presents. My daughter always knows what she is going to get. We go to Smyth Toys Super Store on the day of her birthday, and buy her presents which had been chosen before. I never throw birthday parties for my children. It's just us eating birthday cake from our favorite shop Lidl. We all like chocolate cakes. We have pepsi to drink, which we all like, except John, but normally we don't buy it, because it's too expensive.

Next in line is our wedding anniversary. The best celebration I have with John is when he was banned from driving. We met up in Walsall Town Center, and he bought me a pair of shoes from Duchman. Black high heels 5th Avenue brand. Usually I just give him a card, and he gives me nothing.

Mothering Sunday is celebrated in March too. One time in Church where we were going before, because we used to live in different area Priest called all mothers to the Altar at the end of the Mass, and give us beautiful cards with St. Mary on it. Just after Emilia had been born John with Pawel build a pram for her, so I could take her for the walks. That was special to me. And last year for the first time I got a present from my son. It was a beautiful blouse navy blue with pattern on it.

Easter we celebrate in Jamaican style. John always buy Jamaican bun, and Jamaican, special cheese to eat together with bun. It's delicious. He fries fish. Last Easter we ate fish with festival (it's like a sweet, soft dumpling). I made potato salad, which is Polish speciality, but my husband doesn't like it. We might go for a walk if the whether is good. That's all about our Easter. Jesus had died, and was buried for our sins. On the third day he was risen to life. It's so difficult to explain to Emilia the difference between what we celebrate on Easter, and what on Christmas. On Christmas Jesus is a tiny baby born in a manger, and on Easter he is a grown up man dying on the cross. I hope the older she will be the more she will understand.

In June there is Father's Day. John gets cards from children, with the best wishes.

Ewa's birthdays are the most stressful. Although she is 18 years old she puts so much pressure to get the most expensive present, and a lot of snacks, which I never get. Sadly her two last birthday she spend in the hospital, because of her autism.

Emilia loves Halloween, and I started to like it too. So far we went treat or tricking with all my children only once. Emilia was so excited. She ate all her treats straight away in one go. She was wearing light up witch dress.

November is the month to remember those who died in WW1, and WW2. A lot of people wear a poppy brooch including MPs, royal family, journalists, and also ordinary people as a symbol that we remember about those who have lost their live in these two wars.

In November there are two birthdays: Pawel's, and mine. Pawel is not fussy when it comes to his birthday. He just buys present for his grandmother's money. Birthday cake, pepsi, and I make him potato salad. I always get a nice, expensive present from my husband like watch, or earrings. Cake from Lidl, Pepsi, and I'm ready for another year of my life.

Christmas is the craziest holiday of all. Craziness starts at the beginning of December with so called 'black Friday'. There are a lot of reductions of prices in shops. In some of them customers are actually queuing in front of shopping centers from 4 o'clock in the morning just to be first to get the bargain. We start to buy Christmas presents 2-3 weeks before Christmas. These presents usually are: trainers, clothes, cds, perfume, books, hand bags for me, and quite expensive toys for Emilia, those which need batteries, and are moving, and talking. Of course I get some money from Poland too for Christmas. When it comes to meals John makes some meat baked from the oven like turkey, and pork. I make potato salad, and bake two cakes like chocolate cake, and cake called 'zebra', which is half chocolate, and half vanilla. We eat fish on Christmas Eve in the evening, and the same day we open our presents. On Christmas Day in the morning I prepare special breakfast with tea from the pot, salad, boiled eggs, gherkins, ham, and cheese. After breakfast we eat cakes, and drink pepsi. We might go for a walk if the weather is good. Afterwards John serves us his special dinner. Next day of Christmas is Boxing Day. Nothing special is going on that day. We go to the nearest supermarket Asda to see what they have there. There is no food left in the house, because we don't cook that much. Jesus was born in a manger, because there was no place for Mary, and Joseph in an inn. That is more appealing to Emilia, and easier to understand than Easter message.

John's birthday day is between Christmas, and New Year's Eve. There were years when he didn't celebrate it at all, because he wasn't in a mood. I try to bake cake for him, because he likes home made food. From time to time he was getting nice presents from me too like trainers, or hoodies. But he doesn't like his birthday.

At the very end of each year is New Year's Eve. Only one time since we are in England we did something special that day. It was before Emilia was born. John took us to Birmingham City Centre to welcome a New Year with the crowd, which was gathered there. We had our champagne with us. Otherwise we stay at home watching celebrations of New Year's Eve on television from London.

I love Church. At the beginning I was struggling to adjust to Church services here. I didn't even know the words of prayers, and the songs in English language. But now I'm used to that.

The only annoying thing in my church is that I cannot access confession so easily, and there is only one Church service on Sunday early in the morning while in Poland there are many Church services on Sunday, and confession is during every mass.

Ewa, and Pawel took Holly Communion in Great Britain. They had that sacrament at the beginning of primary school. But Emilia wasn't christen yet. Somehow we cannot organize that with John. She has to be christen as soon as possible, because soon she will have to prepare for her sacrament of First Holly Communion.

Before she was going to Catholic primary school, but not any more. I later applied for school which is nearer to our house, which in not Catholic. It's actually a very nice, big school. There are a lot of things to do outside. I like Emilia's teacher.

Emilia knows already so many things. She is super clever. We all are so proud of her. She adores going to school where she has got many friends.

I was once in Church of England on the mass a long time ago. They don't give Holly Communion there. They don't listen to the Pope. Pope only rules Catholic Church from Vatican. He is our Holly Father.

One time during my confession here priest asked me who was my favorite saint. I said St. Mary.

I like to pray on my rosary a lot. I also pray sometimes from the book, but somehow I don't read Bible any more.

Old Testament is complicated. I know New Testament better.

I wish my children were religious too to know right from wrong.

When I was small I was persecuted, because I was going to Church. I was the only member of my family who regularly attended Church Services. I was of course also praying at home too.

My parents didn't like, and they still don't like Church. They like to hear on news controversy about Church, because they are not into it. Jonh is the same.

'Priests are abusing boys, and girls'. That's what they want to hear.

I believe in celibacy in Catholic Church. If priests had their own families they wouldn't put a 100% into their Churches.

I know there are cases of abuse by priests which is horrible. They should be punished like ordinary people. But majority of priest are doing great job helping people all over the world.

I cannot imagine my life without Church. It means a lot to me.

I'm not perfect. I respect people who don't go to Church. But I don't like being laughed at for going to Church by my parents, or John. It's out of order, and disrespectful. They should be happy for me.

John as a little boy was going to Church every Sunday. He also had lessons from Sunday school. His grandparents were very religious. They brough John up. Now he doesn't go to Church at all. Of course he blames me for that. He says I have discouraged him from going to Church, and my family.

Jamaican Church is more lively. People sing, dance, and clap their hands. That's the Church my John is used to. In Poland parishioners only listen, and sing. That's what I am used to. Even during funerals Jamaicans sing, dance, and clap. They celebrate life of a dead person, not his death. In UK is the same in Church as in Poland. Only language id different.

Life can be full of difficult moments. It's better to have faith to avoid, or deal with them. There is saying in Poland: 'when you are scared you turn to God'. It might be a little too late for that then.

I don't feel better then the other people who don't go to Church. I just wish everybody have the same support which I have, and be happy to have God in my heart.

CHAPTER 14

While we were still in Poland with children I got a worrying phone call from John. He had accident at work. He wasn't in the hospital, so it wasn't that serious, but still I was worried about him. I wanted to see him. By this time John was living in a flat in Croydon.

So for the second time we had left Poland with children, and went to England. I was excited to see John after all these long months of separation. I had quitted my job, and children had quitted Polish school.

I liked this flat in Croydon. It was situated on the 1st floor in the heart of Croydon. There was living room with kitchen, and small bedroom. There was a huge mall nearby. I was happy about it. I always like malls. Just to be close to shops to get a bargain.

Kids' school was close too from our flat. Only park was far, so we didn't go there that often. We didn't have a car back then. John was going to work by tram.

It was good to be with John again. Very good.

Our flat was so tiny. Ewa, and Adam were sleeping in the only bedroom in one, big bed, and we with John on the mattress in our kitchenette on the floor.

We were happy. In London prices of flats to rent are high. Much higher than anywhere else in the UK.

Every Saturday we were going to Lidl by taxi to do our grocery shopping.

John liked his job. I wasn't even thinking to look for one for myself. I was just concentrating on children, to take care of them, and the house.

In my free time I was very often to the local library to use computer, because we didn't have one back then.

I like libraries. Before when internet wasn't so popular you could get a lot of information from librarians.

Most of the time on the computer in this library in Croydon I was reading Polish portal called 'Pudelek' full of gossip about Polish, and foreign celebrities. I remember my grandmother used to like gossip like that when she was alive.

I was also listening to music at home on my radio, when children were at school, and watching television.

There was nice playground next to my children's school. When the weather was good we go there, so they could play. They were going to school called Parish Primary School. It was Church of England school. I even once went for a mass to nearby Church like that.

Life without a work wasn't difficult to me. Ewa, and Pawel were still little. We had enough money to survive. I wasn't interested in getting a job. John didn't expect him to do so either. I was a home maker, and it suited me.

London is great. We still go there from time to time. My husband's two brothers live there, but he doesn't contact them. John used to work on buildings in the City Center, and he is proud of it.

John's time of being banned from going to Poland was up (because of deportation). Somehow 5 years passed which weren't easy for us. I don't know why, but we started to think about going to live in Poland in my grandfather's house in Lodz, who had died a few years before. His house supposed to be mine, but my father had papers for it.

We just wanted to live somewhere to avoid paying rent, which was killing us in London. We didn't know that it was going to be a big mistake. A very big one.

Because John was illegal in England he had to go first to Jamaica to get visa in Polish Embassy to enter Poland.

He got a lot of money from work, because he had been fired from it.

So John went to Jamaica, and we with children were taken by my brother by car to Poland to my parents' house again. Thomas didn't want to take a lot of our things although there was space in the car. We just took TV, radio, and clothes. Our flat had been rented furnished. That was good. At least we didn't have to leave behind our furniture.

John got his visa without any problems. He quickly came to join us in Poland.

I was working in a pharmacy in heath center at that time. I quickly quitted this job, and we went to Lodz by train. It's far from where my parents live. We were travelling the whole night.

My father prepared documents for us to live in this house for free.

We met up with my parents in this house. We were not only ones to live there. On the other side of the house lived Derek. He had been taking care of grandfather before he died. After my grandfather's death Derek still were living there. By the time we arrived he was living there with his girlfriend, and their little daughter. We were sharing bathroom with them.

Everywhere around this house Derek kept broken cars, and dangerous dogs.

The neighborhood wasn't nice there. It is not far from city center.

John quickly found job there in construction company. We applied for permit for him to stay in Poland legally.

I couldn't find a job for myself there although I was in my country.

Ewa started school in Lodz, but Pawel was still at home with me.

I really felt badly there. We didn't have a car. John was going to work by tram. We even didn't have central heating in this house.

Every morning we were going with children to school we were scared of these dogs.

Bathroom was small, and we had to share washing-machine.

Basically everything was wrong about this place. Very wrong.

Now when I think about it I wonder how my parents allowed us to live in a place like that. And again I have to think about racism. They didn't wish me well, since I had been with John. It's sad, but true.

The only good thing which happened to us in Lodz was John getting his permit to stay in Poland. Nothing else.

I remember walking there, looking at other flats, and houses, and being jealous that people had central heating.

We moved in at the beginning of September. In October cold weather stroke. We bought electric heater, but it wasn't enough to heat up the whole house.

John enjoyed his work, and money was good.

We didn't need this experience. We knew better. We should have stick to better.

Schools in Poland are not like those in UK. In Poland you have to pay for everything what children use at school. They don't get nothing for free. It's also required to pay for insurance. That was a big expense for us in Lodz to send Ewa to school.

Generally speaking England is 100% better than Poland. That's what I know. Coming back to Poland was a big mistake. We didn't want to pay rent, and that's what we got. Fortunately we didn't stay long in Lodz. First I had left with children coming back to my parents house. John followed us a few weeks later.

So many times I we ended up in my parents' house since my relationship with John.

Love is great between man and a woman, and can forget everything. I guess it happens sometimes that you run away, when you don't know what to do.

Every move you make you leave your things behind, and that's not good. Later on you have to buy them back. Especially when you have children. They won't switch from one school to the other just like that. It must have been difficult situation for them. Children are not objects. Every time we moved I felt sorry for them. Fortunately they were healthy.

Unlike me. My mental health problem returned around that time. I had to go to see psychiatrist, and she put me on medications. I was diagnosed with bipolar disorder. Thankfully it didn't stop me from doing my every day duties. Since that time I have been on medications for bipolar disorder.

Last year I was in mental hospital for five weeks. It was terrible experience. It started at home. About three days I was acting weird. Nobody couldn't help me. My husband took me to the nearest mental hospital. The problem was that I didn't want to go inside. Some body called the Police to force me in. I took of my clothes. John witnessed all of that. Finally I was inside Dorothy Pattison Hospital.

I cannot remember what was happening with me next.

When I started to come back to my senses I was in different hospital locked in a room with a bathroom with a little window. I couldn't come out of this room. I had no clue what was going on around me. I wasn't wearing my clothes. Things that I was wearing were somebody else's clothes.

One day in the morning doctors came, and asked me if I want to come out of this room. I said 'yes'.

It occurred that I wasn't in Dorothy Pattison Hospital any more. I was in a different hospital far from home.

These things were happening in the middle of corona virus pandemic. No visitors were allowed in any hospitals then.

John came once to visit, but because of that he couldn't go inside. Thankfully I was in lounge area with television then, and one of the patients showed me John through the window. She said: 'look, your husband is here'. He showed me what he brough for me. The most important thing was my mobile. A few minutes later I got from care assistant my things from John. Of course I couldn't keep nothing in my room including phone charger. I only could keep my phone. That was annoying. Even my Coke, and Mars bars they put in their locker, and I had to ask if when I wanted to drink, or eat them. It was dark when John came.

Since then I was holding my mobile phone in my hands like the only hope, and the biggest treasure. I was waiting for somebody from my family to call me. I couldn't call, because I didn't have credit on my phone. I could call from hospital mobile phone.

I had no idea that I had been in there such a long time. Somebody from the staff told me it was already November.

I hated this hospital. I had had to ask for simple things over, and over again until I got them.

I kept refusing medication they were trying to give me. I didn't know who was a nurse, and who was a doctor, and who was a health care assistant.

John, and Melania were calling me whenever they could. I was waiting for these calls. They kept me alive.

Nobody was telling me how much longer I would have to stay there.

Medicine were making me drowsy. That's why I didn't want to take them. I couldn't recognized when there was a day, and where there was a night. I slept a lot nights, and days. I so desperately wanted to come out of this place.

One day somebody from the staff (handsome looking young man) told me that I would be moved somewhere else, closer to home. I finally saw the light in a tunnel. I got ready. It was going to happen in the morning at 11 o'clock. Ambulance was parked by the door in lounge area. They gave me back my charger, and I was ready to go. There were two women in an ambulance with me. I asked them where am I going. One of them checked in a paper work, and said' Dorothy Pattison Hospital in Walsall'. These words were like music to my ears. That was exactly what I wanted to hear.

It was so good to see my psychiatrist from Dorothy Pattison Hospital after I had got there. John enable me to top up my phone. After two nights there I was discharged. I had packed my things in a little suitcase, and health care assistant showed me a way out of the hospital.

My husband was waiting for me outside. He helped me with the suitcase. It was quite early. Children were still at school. He asked me what do we do next. I said 'full English'. It means full English breakfast, which John likes so much. I didn't want to go home yet.

He took me to his favorite place in Pelsall for that breakfast. Later on he told me to buy dye to my hair. I bought it in our Asda. At home first thing John did was to dye my hair, and gave me a nice bath. Ane then I went to bed.

John took one week off work to take Emilia to school, and to take care of me. Because of that he lost that job. He had just got a contract just to lose it a few days before. We were devastated. It happened just before Christmas.

We got a special support from social worker Maria. She organized for us access to food bank. She even had asked us what kind of food we like to eat before she brought our food parcel. Not to mention Christmas. Emilia had never received so many presets for Christmas in the whole her life. There was also a little something for Ewa, and Pawel. Maria really helped my family a lot, and she is a very special social worker. Some people are working in the right places, and Maria is one of them. I will never forget her, and what she did for my family. She basically saved our Christmas last year.

Just before Easter this year Ewa, and John had an argument. I think it was Wednesday in a Holly Week. I was at that time in the nearest supermarket. Ewa called me. She told me she was in a Police car parked in front our house. She called the Police, because her father turned of the supply of water while she was having a shower. He wanted her to save electricity. We were about to run out of it, and she was in the shower in his opinion too long.

When I arrived John wasn't at home. Ewa, and two Policemen came inside the house. Ewa was nervous. They explained the situation to me. Basically nothing bad happened. It could have happened in any different home to other family. I told the Policemen that Ewa had been diagnosed with autism five years ago. Situation like that with calling the Police for no reason at all kept happening from time to time. Ewa calmed down a little bit. Policemen left our house.

After about 15 minutes John wanted to enter the house, but because Ewa was scared again, I didn't let him in. He couldn't open the door with his key, because we had pushed my key, and the door had been closed from the inside.

Ewa called the Police again. They came quickly. John was still by the door when they came. I opened the door to them. We were talking, but a long time I didn't let them in. Ewa was sitting in the living-room waiting for what would happen.

I just told my husband to go. He said he had nowhere to go, and he didn't have any money.

This conversation was going on too long. Policemen were clearly fed up with it. They said they had more important things to do. To help people who needed them more than us.

I was fed up too. I wanted to let my husband in, but as soon as I had opened the door a little wider Ewa started to cry out loud.

So I told him to go again. I started to pack his things in suitcases. Clothes, and cosmetics. Police offered him a lift toWalsall Town Centre. Before he was gone he had came to the house for his passport, and other documents.

I chose my daughter over my husband.

It's good that Pawel, and Emilia were at school at that time.

A few days later on Easter Monday in the evening I got a call from John. He wanted to meet up with me. I was very happy about that, because I had been calling him since that bad Wednesday, but he wasn't picking up his phone.

I knew I made a big mistake, and desperately wanted my husband back.

But some things cannot be rebuild. When trust is gone, there is nothing else to be done.

John lives now in temporary accommodation, and waiting to get a flat from Housing Association in Walsall.

It's good we still keep contact with each other, but because of Ewa we don't live together any more.

My older daughter need me, because of her illness. I don't know if she ever be independent. I hope so, but I'm not so sure about that. She has been in hospitals so many times already. Ewa doesn't get on well with people. I'm worried about her future. I don't want to be like me dependent on John, and benefits.

There is a lot things said in news about mental health problems, but some people don't know what they are talking about.

I know. I have mental health problem, and so does my daughter.

Ewa's first children psychiatrist said that we had a special bond with Ewa. She is looking out for me, and I am looking out for her. We understand each other. At some point we even were taking the same medication, but not anymore.

In Poland in nineties I was actually tied to bed for a few days in mental institution. I don't know if they still do that now. I was given injections to help me to get better. After I had regained my consciousness my mother was helping me to do everything like shower, brushing teeth, put on my clothes, brushing my hair in this hospital. After a couple of weeks, when I was ready parents removed me to clinic in Szczecin, which was closer to home. I spent there three months not knowing why I was there. My parents were visiting me twice a week bringing me stuff I liked like sweets, pepsi, and fruits. I missed them a lot.

There were some activities to do in that clinic. I the most enjoyed Church service every Sunday, and praying on my

Rosary with other patients. I was listening to my music on walkman. I liked U2 back then.

I had a few visitors during this three months I spent there. Three of my friends who studied in Szczecin. My boyfriend was nowhere to be seen.

It had to be hard for my parents just like it's hard for us with John now.

I feel like I cannot trust myself any more. I also cannot trust Ewa. One day everything is all right, and the other one she ends up in the hospital.

Ewa is not the only child I have got. I also have little Emilia, and Pawel to take care of.

Somehow when I was in the hospital my family managed without me. John was praising Pawel. He was helping John a lot during that challenging time.

I was so worried about them when I was in the hospital.

My family means a world to me, but I have to take care of myself not to become unwell again.

I am in a good place now. My children are close to me, and that is my success.

We had had our ups, and downs with John. He is difficult to please. But I know he loves me. I love him too. I couldn't cope without his constant support. I have learnt every single thing to do in the house from him. It's priceless these lessons from him.

Now he is not living with us any more, which is weird. I hope it won't affect our relationship.

I chose to live, and take care of Ewa for the time being. John is a big man. He will be all right. I just didn't want Ewa to have to go to the hospital again.

A year ago Ewa had been in mental institution for a few days in Dudley Port. She was complaining about her dad there although he hadn't done anything to her. One day I asked manager there how she was doing. He said that she was doing well, and that she was ready to leave this hospital, and move to community. I didn't know what it meant. I asked him, and he said that Ewa could get a place on her own. They were going to support her in her new place. At first I liked that idea. I thought it might be a chance for her to be independent. She was 18 back then. But later after I had thought things through, I was against it. The reason why I couldn't agree for that was because she was so depended on me. She was more dependent on me than Emilia constantly asking what she should do, what she should eat, and things like that. I just couldn't imagine her living on her own.

That's why a couple months later John left, because they didn't get on well with Ewa on that terrible Wednesday in Holly Week, just before Easter this year.

He didn't want to leave. I have everything on my head, which is not easy for me. Especially dealing with my youngest daughter Emilia, who doesn't listen to me at all. I have to keep repeating the same commands over, and over again. She is difficult to deal with.

Maybe because I'm older that's why it's so hard to bring her up. With Ewa, and Pawel I didn't have any problems. Age might make a difference.

I will never forget what John said one evening when Emilia was a couple of weeks old. I was holding her in my arms, and he said 'what a mistake'. He meant having Emilia in my life. I was so ashamed of myself.

Emilia just after she had been born she was bringing up milk. One evening I had had enough. John was downstairs seeing me running out of the house. I normally never leave the house in the evening. I was running, and crying. Back then my brother was in England. I was running to his flat, but he wasn't there. So I just sat on the bench in the center of Darlaston. I couldn't stop crying. I called my parents in Poland. They told me to come back home. And so I did.

John was so mad with me. He said that if it wasn't for him Emilia would die in her own vomit. Next day we went to see my gp. He increased the dose of my medicine. Thankfully I didn't have to go to the hospital.

Hospitals are the worse option. When you are mentally ill the staff can treat you very badly. Some of them doesn't respect you. They don't treat you like a human being. When I was in a hospital a year ago staff apparently theft my new clothes, and shoes, which John had bought for me. He was so mad with them. That's how people who work in hospitals like that take advantage of poorly patients.

John took me home, and that was great. He had helped me till I fully recovered. At the beginning I was mostly sleeping the whole days, and nights. So I was useless. Then I started to lose my hair. My psychiatrist told me that it was side effects of one of my medications I was taking. He had reduced dose of that medication, and it helped. I had always had such a thick, and nice hair, and than it was not much left hair on my head. I was worried about it, but fortunately situation improved since I had reduced the dose of this drug.

I felt that my mental health was getting worse. I hadn't been to the hospital for 12 years, and out of the sudden I needed hospitalization again. But what can I do? I just have to take care of myself the best I can, and if I feel badly again I will have to accept it.

Everybody says that physical exercises are good for mental heath. I don't do anything like that.

I should try to be more active. Ewa would join me. All we do is to walk to the nearest supermarket to buy some snacks, and come back home. Occasionally we might go to the nearest park.

Pawel is a sportive one in our family. He likes to ride his bike, play football, and basketball.

John only drives.

Now when John doesn't live with us any more we meet without children unless we take them to the park. Ewa never goes with us, because John doesn't want to see her.

She had called the Police on John so many times that he had enough of that. That's why he doesn't want to come back. He doesn't want to have criminal record.

Now my family is split. It was either us with children to leave, or John. So I decided to stay at home with Ewa. John had took his belongings, and left.

On Easter Monday John had came for me, and showed me where he lived. He still lives there. I was surprised. He got a room in Birmingham. It's called temporary accommodation. It's not a bad place. I was so happy that he was all right, and that he still wanted to be in contact with me, and Pawel, and Emilia.

He takes me there from time to time.

John is waiting to get a flat. I hope he won't be waiting too long. In temporary accommodation he has to share kitchen, and bathroom.

He doesn't complain. He is grateful for that chance he had got.

I miss him. We meet each other around two times a week. Emilia always want to see him. Last time she said that Ewa, and John had to apologize to each other. She knows exactly what she is saying. But I wouldn't count on that. It's simply too late. People don't change, and Ewa will live with her health condition till the rest of her life.

The most important is that John hasn't left the country. That was my biggest fear. He has family abroad in Switzerland, USA, and of course in Jamaica.

He just cannot abandon us after these 20 years together. He cares about us, and loves us.

We had already spilt up a couple of times a few times, but like a boomerang we are always back together again. We just cannot be apart.

Because what we have is real. We don't pretend somebody who we are not.

John is such a good father. Even now children are coming back to school after Easter break he is worried if Pawel has had a haircut. He bought poloshirts, and shoes to school for Emilia.

He cannot stop worry about us. That's why I'm glad. I'm not proud of myself for what have we done to John with

Ewa, but maybe, just maybe it will be for a better. I just have to hope, and pray for that.

Everything depends on what kind of flat John will get, and where. If it's a good one he will be happy. And of course the sooner the better.

Not only Ewa used to make John mad. Also Emilia, because she has a big mouth, and she can say anything. Good that at school she behaves herself.

Now when he is gone Emilia desperately wants him back.

Children are ungrateful. They don't appreciate what you as a parent do for them.

It's normal for them. Things have to be done. It doesn't matter who is doing them, and at what cost.

We became parents very quickly with John. We had met in July, and in November that year I was already pregnant.

We hadn't really enough time to get to know each other better, because we had to concentrate on our children.

We didn't plan it.

Now Ewa, and Pawel are almost adults. I has been hoping we could do some good time with my husband. They would be able to babysit Emilia from time to time. Bu she can be difficult to deal with. Only Pawel knows how to approach her. Ewa with Emilia- constant troubles. The same with me.

I am her mum. I should know better. But Ewa also should bear in mind that Emilia is 13 years younger than she. Ewa should let it go sometimes, because Emilia is not going nowhere. She is, and always will be our baby. Ewa is old enough now to be a mother herself.

One of my fiend on Face Book wrote to me one day that children nowadays are different than they had been before. Millenium babies. She has got two children: one boy is at Emilia's age, and the girl is a teenager.

I think is because of technology we have know.

When I was a child there weren't even mobile phones. Kid were paling outside more often.

Now they don't have to go out at all. Everybody, and everything is within hands reach.

At the beginning when my daughter Ewa had introduced me to smart phone I was excited, and so proud that she could use it.

I use it now. I found on Face Book my cousin Ewa from Poland. We had been very close back in the days. We write to each other quite often. She is 10 years older than me. I can write to her about everything.

But what's the point of all this writing when we probably will never see each other again?

I have a few people on Face Book. I'm sorry, but to write to them is just a waste of time. I write only to them, because I only like to write. Instead of that I should talk to somebody in person, or do something with my children (but they are on their phones too).

My mother doesn't use Face Book. It's a shame, because I could sent her quickly some nice pictures of grandchildren if she used Face Book.

All those social media are to show off something. Body, clothes, houses, bags, you name it.

It's a crazy world we live in. A lot of people, especially young ones, can get lost in it.

We are lucky with John. Our children so far stay out of trouble. Ewa tells me everything she does. Pawel is more mysterious.

These few months ahead will be crucial for my two eldest children. Ewa will finish College in a year time, and Pawel Sixth Form. I just wait, and see what they will do with their lives.

I don't want them to go to work they finish education. I hope Pawel will go to university, and Ewa will find for herself a good job.

Whatever they decide to do I'll support them as much as I can.

I cannot do much, because I don't have money, but I think they respect me.

Everybody does what they can. Most of my time I sent with them at home, so they are close me.

They also might fall in love with somebody. I have to be ready for changes like that. Ewa doesn't have a partner yet. Pawel –I don't know.

Ewa told me about a year ago that she is bisexual. She likes boys, and girls. I was surprised, but I said to her that I just wanted for her to be happy in her relationship. Deep down inside I'm hoping it will be a boy she will fall in love in.

John , for example , is homophobic. He doesn't approve of relationship like that. He doesn't know that Ewa is bisexual.

I don't know how it works either. In England the same sex couples can get married. That's what I know.

Because of Ewa's autism she struggles with relationships. Sometimes I'm trying to help her, but it doesn't work. She knows who she likes, and who she doesn't.

What I like about my Ewa that she is self-confident unlike me. I admire that in her character.

Pawel is shy, and he always have some problems dealing with people. He is afraid to make a fool of himself. He also doesn't want me to make a fool of myself. He is very polite, and respectful towards people. I hope in the future people won't take advantage of him, because of his good character.

I think that he is ashamed of his Polish roots. Ewa is not.

At the beginning when we had started to live in UK I was the same. I wanted to be more British than people who lived here the whole of their life.

At the start living in a strange country you just observe people around you. Every country is different, and you need time to adjust to your new life.

I think in England it's easy to do that, because there is a lot of help available.

In my children' primary school they had a translator who helped them from time to time. They could speak English, but they couldn't write in this language.

Even in surgeries you could have translator if you couldn't speak English. I don't know if it's still available.

The most important for a foreigner in a strange country is not to isolate yourself from the rest of people. You just have to come out, and be brave.

To know the language is very important. If you don't know you have to learn it.

There are many different communities in here: Polish community, Jamaican community, Muslim communities, and many more, and we have to somehow live together in peace.

CHAPTER 15

We couldn't make it in Lodz so we had to make it in Swinoujscie, where my parents live.

Father helped us to rent a flat. John found a job in building company. I was working in a pharmacy.

Children went to school close to our flat, and on the way to my work. We didn't have a car. I took children to school in the mornings, and brought them back home after work.

My mother sometimes visited me in my work place in the afternoons after her work. My parents very often were taking us with children by car to promenade, or to the beach for a walk.

John liked his work. He was so proud of me that I was working in that pharmacy. Children also were happy going to that school. They were different, because of their skin colour, and of their height. Ewa, and Pawel were so tall back then. They are still tall, especially Pawel. We are not so tall with John.

I remember when Pawel was playing football for a team all parents were all the time talking about his height. I didn't like that.

My father always asks how tall are my children. Size matters to some people.

We don't live a healthy lifestyle. We eat a lot of sweets, and use a lot of cooking oil.

Only Pawel changed his attitude towards food.

I think everything started with program 'food dudes', which he had at the end of his primary school. Out of a sudden he started to ask me to put some heathy fruits in the boxes, he had got at school. He also started to exercise (he was running up, and down our stairs in the garden). In 2016 when he joined football team he was fit, and skinny.

I'm worried about Ewa, because she just loves food. What would happen if she lived on her own? Now I'm trying to control her when it comes to eating. But I'm bad as well. I don't set an example for anybody. John calls me fat all the time, which he shouldn't. He also had something to hide (big belly).

Although Ewa is fat she doesn't have problem with that. She puts on her clothes in the morning. She does her hair. And she knows she looks good. Of course she would like to lose weight, but for heath reasons only.

When you are a teenager you might have some insecurities when it comes to the shape of your body. I understand that. You want everybody to like the way you look. But when you become woman with a husband you shouldn't have these insecurities any more. Somebody chose you to be your husband. You shouldn't worry about the way you look any more. That's the way I see it.

I think that's the way women want to catch attention talking about these extra kilograms.

I was on the meeting with local weight Watchers a few years ago, and I didn't like it. It's a program to lose weight. They even have their own products in the stores.

I didn't like it. Because it was like a religion to me. Everybody was talking about their diet, temptation, and cravings.

When I was pregnant with Emilia I had had allocated dietician to help me to lose weight. It was strange, because I was pregnant, and instead of gaining weight I was losing it. I dropped one size in trousers. I was proud of myself.

I would like to look good for John. He likes me, but he would like me even more if I lost some weight. If it happens, maybe finally I would hear some compliments from him for a change. He never compliments me. I wish it would be possible, but I don't see it coming any time soon, which is a shame.

Emilia has the same problem like me, and Ewa. I only hope that they won't put her on scale, and send me a letter that she weights too much (at school).

I used to get a lot of them from Ewa's, and Pawel's primary school.

Some people say it's a neglect to overfeed children. Some otherwise have opinion that giving food to children is showing them love.

I always think that sweets are cheap, and that's why I buy them. But fruits are at the same price. Emilia likes fruits too, and the rest of us.

When we do our grocery shopping fruits, and sweets are gone from kitchen cupboards within one day, or two. Only apples stay longer. John is always so mad that we cannot save our favorite things to last us for the whole week. He is used to saving everything he has got. John was brought up in countryside in Jamaica by his grandparents. They had animals, and planted their own vegetables, and fruits. They always have some money saved for rainy days. That's why John is used to that. I always tell him 'God will provide', while John says 'God will provide those who provide themselves'.

The truth is that I love money, and I love to do shopping. If I could I would shop every day.

There are not so many shops in our town. There is only one supermarket, and a few little shops.

We usually go shopping in Walsall. Sometimes to Wolverhampton, West Bromwich, or Birmingham.

The best shopping center in Birmingham is Bull Ring, in Walsall Saddlers, and in Wolverhampton Wulfrun.

I like big shops. I'm trying to avoid the small ones.

John always is trying to support little shops. He doesn't like this big corporations.

He used to own his own shop in Jamaica with food. Because of this experience he doesn't like to work for people any more. He knows he could make it on his own. My mother's shop with herbs, and other medicines was a big inspiration to him. He wanted us to open similar business. But it hasn't happened yet.

I always have to live in my parents' shadow. I cannot be successful like them. My place is a bottom while they are on the top. Always so they can step, and laugh at my family, and me.

How is it possible that your own parents don't wish you well?

I'm just kidding myself that they care.

John knew that from the beginning of our relationship that money mattered to them, and nothing else.

They don't have feelings, and don't care how other people feel.

I remember how happy I was when I met John. I wanted to share my happiness with my parents. But they weren't happy for me at all. It was a problem to me.

My sister-in-law wrote to me recently. My brother betrayed her. They are divorced now. My mother wasn't even bothered to tell off Thomas after what he had done. That's how overprotective she is over my brother. She makes him sandwiches to work although he is 40 years old.

A few weeks ago he got a baby with his new wife. When I talk to my parents they don't even mention this baby.

I know my mother is ashamed of him. It's better to stay faithful to your wife. Otherwise you have to pay the price. But when you don't have morals whatsoever that what happens.

In most religious when you are married you have to stay with your spouse for ever.

In Christianity you cannot have sex before marriage.

Times are changing, but people facing the same challenges.

I had had sex with John before we got married. I did it, because he said 'please', and I thought that he wouldn't like to see me again if I don't do that. First evening we had met, and the other one I was in his bed.

It was so good to be in his arms. I couldn't sleep the whole nights, because I was so happy. I was in my man's arms. He was mine. Nothing else mattered.

I had a time of my life with John in Lausanne after we had just met. We were going clubbing, we were going for long walks along the shore of Geneva Lake, sunbathing, and swimming in this lake.

Lausanne is a picturesquere town. On the other side of Geneva Lake there are French Alps.

John's sister still lives in Switzerland, but not in Lausanne any more. She even visited us a few times in England. She travels a lot all over the world. I'm so jealous of her life style. John likes, and respects very much her husband Francois. They only have one child together. Mario, and Lashawn were born in Jamaica. They have different dads.

Switzerland is a paradise. We wanted to stay in this paradise too with John, but things didn't work out.

In July it will be 20th anniversary of our meeting with John. I wish we could go to Lausanne with children to celebrate that, and show them where we met.

When John complains about me, and our relationship I always tell him 'you was the one to call me'.

Now when Ewa, and Pawel are so grown up I am trying to teach them how it is with relationships. How do I do that? I am not a specialist, but I am doing my best. Thought my own experience, and through experience of my brother.

My favorite show is 'Keeping up with the Kardashians'. I was watching it with Ewa, and Pawel a lot. I was trying to tell my children what is good, and what is bad in this show.

I think that my children (except from Emilia) know already what is good, and what is bad when it comes to relationships. When my brother cheated on his wife they were shocked. I was shocked too.

I am telling to my children that they may have a few relationship, but marriage is for ever. In Catholic Church marriage is a sacrament. You should stay with your spouse for ever.

And again I'm not a good example for Ewa, and Pawel, because we got married with John only in Register Office, not in Church.

We got married in Jamaica. I came there with Ewa, and Pawel especially to marry John. We spent there one month. There was no time to arrange wedding in Church.

Ewa, because of her autism, is struggling with relationship with other people. I was even thinking to go clubbing with her. We both love music. It might be a good idea. Maybe she would meet somebody nice there one day.

I don't drink alcohol at all. On a few occasions I drunk smirnoff vodka. I even drunk that with Ewa recently to introduce her to my favorite alcoholic drink. She liked it. John doesn't drink alcohol either. We are all on medications. He has got coronary heart disease. John takes more tablets than me. Ewa takes one antipsychotic medicine in the morning, and sleeping tablet in the evening. But we have never been told by our doctors that we couldn't drink alcohol, so probably we can.

Alcohol can put you in big troubles if you drink too much. I cannot even imagine how people can be so drunk that they don't remember what they were doing. Five years ago it had happened to John, and he paid big price for it.

He went to the party in private house. Some Polish friends of his invited him. I didn't even know one of them. I was so happy for him to go to that party. I was thinking he deserved some good time.

But he didn't return after the party. I woke up the next day, and he wasn't there(at home).

I will never forget how worried I was. Especially because it lasted the whole day. I was just talking to the Police in the evening that day when John came back home (I wanted to report him missing).

What a relief it was to see him. He didn't look good that Sunday. He just sat on the chair in the kitchen. He said that last night he spent in jail.

He didn't remember anything what happened, but a lot had happened after this party. That's how drunk he was drinking Polish vodka.

John had driven to this party, but he didn't come back by car although he had been trying to do so. He crashed into the wall on the nearby house. Fortunately nobody got hurt including him. Our car was totally crashed. We were going to never see it again being taken by the Police.

Our life changed immediately, because we had lost our car. Childrens' schools were far back then. We had been taking them, and bringing back home by car, but not any more.

Monday morning we were all on the bus taking children to schools. John was in troubles with the Police. Insurance didn't cover the situation our car was damaged.

That's what alcohol can do to people.

The worst case scenario is addiction.

My grandfather, and my auntie from the side of my mother were alcoholics. They are not alive any more.

My auntie was my favorite one. She was my mother's younger sister. She died in tragic circumstances not letting her family call the ambulance when she felt bad (she couldn't breath properly). Her son found her dead in the corridor at night. Even my mother was speaking to her over the phone that tragic evening to persuade her to get help. But what you can do over the phone 700 km away?

My mother, and my auntie were close. I wasn't at the funeral due to luck of money.

John was in court, because of this accident. He was banned from driving for 1.5 years, and had to do drink-driving course.

Life without a car is possible. A lot of people own cars, and can drive.

It's harder to get a job when you don't drive. First question when you are looking for a job is if you drive, and have a car. Employers want you to be flexible, and be able to work different shifts.

It's an additional skill.

My husband without a car felt 'less than a man'. I felt sorry for him. He had to take three buses to get to work, and three to come back. It took him altogether 4 hours to commute in both ways.

Our flat in Swinoujscie was on the second floor. Rent was expensive. I didn't like our life in Poland. Something wasn't right. My husband didn't complain, but I just missed England. Nothing was holding back there. Children were complaining about their school. Pawel even heard N-work at school.

I didn't like my job, because my work colleague constantly was calling me fat. John was proud of me working in my field, but I deep down inside felt uncomfortable there. I just did't remember anything exciting about my life there.

I was too dependent on my parents, and John didn't like that.

The way my parents treat me now is different, because finally I have my own opinion. I'm free from their opinions. I know what to do myself without anybody telling me what to do. I am happy about that. It had taken me so many years to get to that point. I have my own family from the longest time, and I have to take care of them. I know how to do that. Nobody has to tell me how any more.

We were blessed with John with three children. Thankfully they are quite healthy, and they haven't given us any problems yet.

My parents like to interfere in my life. That's why I'm so happy that we live far from them now. They cannot interfere any more.

I will have to stop calling my parents so often. I basically still tell them everything about our life. Father likes to laughs at me all the time, because he is a joker. Mother laughs too.

The truth is that all these years they have been sending money to me from time to time. But it doesn't give them rights to laughs at me.

At the beginning my mother sent us money for laptop in 2010 so we could buy our own, first laptop. She sent over £300. When Ewa was in the hospital I got money to fix our car. It was also around £300, or even more.

I got a lot of money from my parents over all these years.

When we were going to visit them in Poland they were the ones to pay for our tickets always.

Yes, my mother, and father are generous. I cannot deny it.

I'm used to this additional support. Thanks to them I can treat myself, and the children sometimes.

Now when they are sending it's a smaller amount. I think it's because my mother works part time now. Besides they have to help my brother financially, because he has to pay now child maintenance to his ex-wife. And they have more grandchildren. Thomas has now 2 months old baby boy called Julek. So we are not the only ones.

When I talk to my parents over the phone I talk a lot about us. Maybe that's too much. Maybe that's why they don't want to talk to me?

I should ask more questions about them maybe. I keep calling them, and almost every time I get hurt. The reasons why is like that, because they are the ones to end our conversation. Too busy to talk while I'm enjoying myself. I cannot do nothing to change it. Obviously it's a waste of time to talk to me for my parents. I am not rich. They must be afraid that every day I call them I want money from them. That's my theory.

My children always give me advise not to call my parents that often. They don't want me to be hurt, and complain again.

But I cannot help myself. It's like a bad habit.

At the end of 2009 John talked to his sister Margaret. We were living in Poland then. She told him that her two older children Mario, and LaShawn lived, and studied in UK. She had rented them a house in Walsall in West Midlands.

John was so shocked how cheap their rent was. It was nothing like London prices which we had paid before.

Because we both with my husband missed England we decided to visit his nephew, and niece in Walsall for a few days. I had already been to Walsall, but John hadn't.

Ewa, and Pawel stayed with their grandparents. We took a bus from Szczecin to Birmingham. Of course, as I had already mentioned before, in Calais, on the border between France, and England we were stopped by immigration. Our Polish bus didn't wait for us. After a few hours they let us go. We took ferry from Calais to Dover. From Dover we travelled by English bus National Express. Fortunately we didn't have to pay for it.

Mario, and LaShawn were waiting such a long time for us in Birmingham Coach Station.

John is always stopped on the boarders. He says that it happens, because he is black. A lot of black people still smuggle drugs through the boarders. Even my son once was searched by the Police Officer in the evening next to our library.

John's nephew, and niece took us by bus to their house. It was evening already when we arrived at our destination. We'd eaten some fast food from the nearest restaurant, and went to bed tired after the journey.

I like Mario, and LaShawn. Mario is calm. LaShawm is very lively. They like children a lot.

We spent a few days with them. They were students at Walsall College. Mario studied computers, and LaShawn childcare.

We liked Walsall with John. It was so good to be back to England.

We opened a bank account in a bank. We made the decision to move to the house where Mario, and LaShawn lived.

It was a three bedroom house with living-room, and front room. There were enough space for all of us. Of course we were going to move in with our children.

Woman from the bank gave us a good advice about what kind of benefits we should apply for. Before in London we had never got any benefits from the government. Not even Child Benefits.

In Poland, and Jamaica there were no benefits at all back then.

Some people in Britain say that benefits are good. Some don't think so.

My family has already got a lot of help from the state, and we are still getting.

John was always working, but on low income. I wasn't working a lot because of my illness.

Children most of this time have had free school meals. We all are getting medicines, dental care, and optician for free. Now Ewa has free buss pass to get to College, and free school meals. Emilia, and Pawel have free school meals too.

Ewa, and Pawel get bursary payments (it's like a pocket money).

I'm not against benefits, but I understand the reasons why people can be against it.

You can get used to this type of lifestyle on benefits. No work, and free money.

People who go to work every day can be frustrated. They pay their taxes, and thanks to them we get benefits.

But some people have never been on low income. Some people have never been hungry, and used food bank.

In 2016 Great Britain had referendum whenever to stay, or leave United Europe. People voted to leave.

We think with John that the reason why they voted like that it's because there were too many foreigners in UK, and British people were fed up with them. These foreigners were taking their jobs, and benefits.

CHAPTER 16

We didn't spend a lot of time in Swinoujcie. One year only. Ewa, and Pawel during that year had learnt how to write in Polish language.

John had came to Walsall earlier. We fallowed him a few weeks later.

That's the way we used to live. Always on the move. Never settled. Looking for something, but not sure for what.

Everybody wants to be happy I guess. Happiness can be many different things. It depends on the person.

Sometimes when couple split up they say 'we want different things from life'. John, for example, very often says 'we have nothing in common'. But we complement each other. I think we are perfect match. We cannot live without each other. We prove it over, and over again.

So many times we used to make our way from Poland to England by bus. The biggest exactment is always on the ferry from Calais to Dover. When we are close to the shore of Dover, when I can call John from my mobile, when there is my network coverage Vodafone.

I love these ferries. Especially when I can buy something in the shops. My heart beats faster when we pass cliffs of Dover. I'll meet my husband soon.

Maidstone, London, Coventry, and here we are in Birmingham. Tired after 24 hours journey, but extremely happy. Is my husband already there waiting for us on the bus stop? He is always there. That's what I like about him. He never disappoints me. He has big mouth, he can say anything, but he never fails when it comes to important moments in our life.

I believe in what people say. That's why I got mad with him sometimes. He never apologizes so I cannot count on that. Maybe one day I will finally hear from him that he is glad that we met. John always says that I'm different than anybody else. Unique. I don't know if it is a compliment, or not.

I cannot compare. He had had many women in his life before me. I'm not so experienced as him in relationships.

Our life in Walsall I had to start with arranging schools for children. It wasn't so difficult. I just went to the Council, and they told me what to do. I managed to apply for primary school for my kids. Quickly we were offered places in the nearest primary school from our house.

There were a lot of Muslim people living there. I didn't mind. I don't observe people like John does. I only was telling to my children not to say bad things about other people in Polish language. I think it's disrespectful to use foreign language to chat bad things about the others. That's just not right. Or to pretend that you cannot speak English to avoid troubles.

When we had to travel by taxis to Lidl in Walsall to do grocery shopping when John was banned from driving I asked the driver (who was originally from Pakistan) how he could speak English so well, and what was his first language. He said that foreigners who come from this part of the world to UK have to learn English before they start to work, and successfully pass the test.

In my opinion it's a very good approach.

When you cannot speak the language in a country you live in you are isolated.

I saw that in case of my ex sister-in-law. They came with my brother to live in UK a few years after us. Maria couldn't speak English. Thomas could.

She had been happy here until she had a baby. She is not like me. Maria likes to talk to people, and here she couldn't do that.

They were gone quickly from England, because of her. Thomas didn't want to go nowhere, bus she insisted. He listened to his wife. Now they are after divorce.

I had had my English lessons since Year 2 of primary school. There were private lessons. My father was working abroad as a sea man so he knew how important English language was. He could speak English, but not any more.

I also learnt French language for 1 year. These were private lessons too. I had a very good French teacher, but I don't use it any more so it's forgotten.

At primary school in my times we were learning Russian language, because I was growing up in communist times, and Russia was our big brother.

I wanted to study English language at the university, but I wasn't successful to get a place on that course.

I was always into books, and magazines, and music. That what was interesting to me, and still interests me now. I love to read. Now when I live in a strange country I read biographies of famous people. I like to know who is who.

I started with Katie Price's books first. My mother couldn't believe that a model can actually write books. She has a couple of autobiographies, and also fiction books. I believe that she had written them. I can relate to her, because she also has autistic child. His name is Harvey, and he is 18 now. Just like my Ewa. So me, and Katie have something in common.

She had been married a few times, and I think because of Harvey her husbands left her.

Very often it happens that when there is ill child in the family parents split up, and mother has to face this challenge alone to rise this child.

I also read Coleen Ronney 'Coleen's real style'. She is a wife of famous footballer Wayne Ronney(now he is a couch I guess). It's a book about fashion. What to wear on certain occasions.

I like Coleen. They have four children together. Four boys. They were with Wayne childhood sweethearts (it means that they were a couple in Secondary school already).

She has been through a lot with him, but they are still together. That's what I admire in certain women that they can forgive, and forget (wrongdoings of their husbands). Family, and children should always come first. Children don't understand why married couples split up. They blame themselves for that. Children are innocent.

I follow celebrities' life style, because I don't have real friends.

When I was a little girl I was actually talking to women in my mother's magazines about fashion.

I was interested in life of Kerry Katona, because she is bipolar like me. I read book about her.

Amanda Holden biography was interesting too. We used to watch with children series 'Wild at heart' with this actress. I think she is very preety, and always look good.

Of course I had to read books about Beyonce, and Rihanna, who are my favorite singers.

Mariah Carey has just released her memoir. I don't have it yet. She is the one who I was listening to on my walkman at night. I was also dancing to her songs (my favorite song from these times when I was teenager was 'Fantasy').

I don't know why, but I always prefer female singers now.

Before it was different. I was a big fan of INXS, and U2. I was even on U2 concert in Warsaw in Poland. Sadly Michael Hutchence, front man from INXS committed suicide. I was devastated when my mother told me that news one morning.

One day I bought a new album of U2 in Morrisons. It's not my cup of tea any more. I don't like rock music any more. I prefer RNB, and POP music now.

Ewa loves music too. Her favorite artist is Chris Brown.

Music helped her to go through tough times in hospitals she'd been to.

John had already working by the time we arrived from Poland. He worked with many Polish people as a welder.

Of course he didn't complain about his job, but some days he got a flash in his eyes from another welder, and he was in pain the whole night afterwards. His workplace wasn't safe to work, because they didn't have special screens separating one welder from another.

He was earning good money there. Sometimes he even did overtime on Saturdays.

We still lived with John's nephew Mario. We shared with him rent, and bills. Mario's sister LaShawn wasn't living in this house any more. She had a boyfriend in Switzerland (now they are married), and, I guess, she missed him. She was only 16 back then.

It was a three bedroom house with living-room, and front room. We were sleeping with John in a front room. Children upstairs in those there bedrooms with Mario. John had bought them new beds from Argos before we came.

Mario was young too. He was always on his laptop playing one computer game all the time (I don't know which one). When he wasn't playing this game he was watching TV kids channels. He was a role model for our children.

Mario is very easy-going person, patient, and he likes children. We were lucky to live with somebody like him.

Every Monday John was giving me pocket money (£20). When children were at school I was often walking to the Town Center of Walsall. It was taking me about half an hour to get there. I liked Walsall more, and more. I liked to be in the center of that town.

I even had one friend. Children told me that in their school there was Polish boy called Kryspin. Somehow I started to talk to his mother. Her name was Gosia (we are still friends).

She had came to England a few months earlier than us. It was good to have somebody to talk to. She couldn't speak English. Very often I was helping her. I was translating for her. We were going to dentist, or surgery together.

She was also helping me by collecting my children from school from time to time.

I used to visit her for coffee. We were going for walks to the nearest parks together with our children. Children were playing football together.

Gosia was my first friend, and sadly the only one. I didn't know that it would be like that. Now we live far from each other. We keep in touch via FaceBook.

Thanks to that we were living with Mario we didn't pay so much for rent. We had more money to spend. I was always looking forward to Fridays when we were doing grocery shopping in Morrisons. We had a car then – Ford Mondeo.

First thing we bought was TV to our room. John bought me hair dryer, and straightener in Argos. I was happy about that.

My favorite shop back then was The Works with books, and stationary equipment. I'm childish. I like things like that. I bought there for children 'Bible Stories', and 'My first prayers'. For myself first book I bought in that shop was 'Angel Uncovered' by Katie Price. Kids got big skateboards, and big bikes.

Life was good. It felt like we were in the right place.

I quickly got my first job through work agency First Personnel in Dudley. The place of my work was Wednesbury. I had to take one bus there. It took me about 10 minutes to get there by bus.

It was work in a warehouse packing cds, films(dvds), and games (nintendo, or computer games). The job was easy. We were most of the time working on conveyor belt putting cases on cds, or placing stickers.

There were many foreigners working there including Polish people. I had a Polish friend like Gosia, who couldn't speak English, and I had to translate for her too. But after a few weeks we didn't talk to each other any more so I was on my own again.

It's nice to have somebody to talk to on your breaks from work.

In warehouses, or factories most of people who work there are men. I like to talk to women rather than men. Women have different topics than men.

I stayed in that job one and a half years. All these time I was working not every day of the week. Usually it was three days a week. I was satisfied with that. At least I had my own salary. And I didn't have to ask John for money. He still paid the rent, and our grocery shopping.

I left this job because at the end of my time there they were calling me to come to work. I was buying ticket for a bus, and when I got there they simply were saying: 'sorry, no job today', which was terrible. Everybody had their own plans. They didn't treat us right any more.

I didn't know then that this job was the longest which I ever do.

I had to quit it. No way I could stand this treatment any more.

Around that time my depression started, because I couldn't find another job. Basically I was getting up in the mornings to prepare children to school. I was taking them to school, and after coming back home I was going straight to my bed. It was hard to leave my bed to make myself some breakfast.

Around two o'clock in the afternoon I was starting to cook some dinner. I was bringing kids from school, and I was happy to have company again. I could forget in the afternoon, when children accompanied me, about my bad thoughts when I was alone most of the day in bed.

I am pharmacy technician with qualification gained in Poland. My place of work should be in a pharmacy, not in a warehouse, or factory. I have never registered with General Pharmaceutical Council to work as a pharmacy technician in England, which is required to do so. That's why I could only work in pharmacy as a pharmacy assistant. This position you can get without any qualifications.

I had been looking for a job in pharmacy, but without any success. That's what was bringing me down. I felt like a such a failure. John as a welder was working hard, and I even couldn't help the situation.

I don't know why I couldn't find a work in a pharmacy? Maybe I didn't try hard enough.

I had been to many interviews, but they never called me back with job offer. One time they called me from one pharmacy only to tell me that I was unsuccessful.

I really wanted to go to work. I wanted John to be proud of me.

My friend Gosia wasn't working either. Maybe that's why we got on so well being in similar situations. Her husband comes from Poland too.

I really enjoyed visiting her in the mornings for coffee. She had Polish television.

Later on she fell pregnant. So many times I was going to the Manor Hospital for check ups. I even was with her that day when her son Josh was born. Her mother had came from Poland to help her with a baby.

I was jealous. I wanted to be pregnant too, but I didn't want it to happen in the house we lived in.

The problem with our house was that we had old windows. They should have to be changed, but our Estate Agency hadn't done that (we had never asked to do so).

It was so hard to heat up the house in cold months. We were putting so much credit on our gas card, and still it wasn't enough. Boiler was also very old.

After Mario had left we had to pay full rent, and all bills ourself.

I remember when I was cooking dinners I was actually praying not to run out of gas (we had gas cooker) to be able to finish.

We had the whole house to ourselves after Mario had left.

I wasn't working long months so quickly we begun to struggle. We were receiving Child Tax Credit, and Child Benefits. John was on a low income. We didn't know anything about any housing association back then.

At the end of the year 2012 I got a job in Bescot to wrap sheets of paper. It was also job through work agency

(Contract Options). I was doing night shifts. I was walking to work in the evenings, and coming back home in the early mornings (my shift was finished at 5 am).

It wasn't a difficult job. Just to deal with paper, and put these packages on the pallets. My work colleges couldn't even write in English (they were Polish too).

I had been happy, but my happiness didn't last long. I lasted there six weeks only. They fired me just before Christmas.

Another unnecessary experience which brought me down. I was back to my shell unemployed to hide from the rest of the world.

I just take things too hard. Shiet happens. Some people understand that, but I don't. If it's not my way it's no other way.

I was devastated to lose that job. What was wrong with me?

First of all it's hard to find job for me. And when I get it I lose it quickly.

Children always came for money to me, because they are closer to me than to John. And I had to ask John for the money for them, which I don't like.

No matter if it's a pound, or a hundred pounds. It's hard.

Before we had a joint bank account with John. We had two debit cards. One for me, and the other one for him.

John got paid on Thursdays. I always was looking forward to this day of the week. I never knew how much money he would leave me to spend in the bank. He was withdrawing most of it in the mornings before work.

I was taking children to school on Thursdays. First thing after we had left the house we were going to the nearest cash machine to check how much money there was left for me to spend by John. After I had dropped children to school I was going to Morrisons to spend the money for sweets, magazines, cds and things like that. That's the only time I felt well doing my Thursday shopping.

On Fridays we did with John grocery shopping which I like to do too. For dinner that day we always had fast food from the nearest restaurant called 'Dixy'. We loved chicken wraps there with fries.

One day we were in real troubles. Bailiffs came to our house. During the long period of time before we were getting letters in red writing from them. I didn't know who bailiffs were. We hadn't paid parking ticket with John (£40). It raised up to £900 after all these months of not paying it. That was the money we owned them. If we didn't pay them they would take all our belongings from our house, and we would still own them some money.

I had never opened the door to anybody before, but this bad day he was waiting for us in the car. After we had came back home with children the man followed us, and knocked at the door. I wasn't going to open, but he said 'I know you are inside Mrs.... 'and he said my surname. I had to open.

He wanted this big amount of money immediately. I called John, who was at work. I couldn't get through to him. The man left our house. He was supposed to come back the same day. John returned from work. We hid our expensive things, but the man didn't returned. Instead of that he called me, and said to make arrangement with head office.

That was so scary. I quickly wrote a letter to head office, and they agreed for me to pay £20 a week. It was such a relief

Sometimes my husband's cousin Patricia came to visit us. She is such a nice, positive person. Full of energy, which is contagious. They even gave us one day with her husband Phill their pieces of furniture.

She is the one why we live in Walsall.

It was nice to get those visits from her. She didn't work any more, because of some health problems.

Now she is very ill. I think she has got dementia.

John sometimes goes to her house to help Phill with some work.

Sadly I don't see Patricia any more.

I don't know why, but John doesn't like to go to people's houses. So many times Patricia had been inviting us for Sunday dinner, but we never came. John never took us there.

The same problem is with our elderly neighbors. John always parks his car in front of their house.

They were so good to us throughout all these years. Their names are Graham, and Jean. They gave us so many things including sweeties, potatoes, meat. One morning on Easter Sunday Jean brought us a card with £10in it. When Ewa was in the hospital last time Jean also gave me a get well card with some money in it for Ewa. I took it to the hospital my daughter was in.

Last time I talked to Jean she told me that she was in constant pain. District nurse was coming to her every week. She was using morphine patches. Her oncologist was from New Cross Hospital in Wolverhampton. According to this information she must have cancer.

First time we talked for such a long time. She will be 81 this year.

Soon Jean, and her husband will be moving out to the bungalow somewhere close to where their son lives.

I bought for her a vase in Wilko for their new place. First time they got something from us for a change. I hope she likes it.

CHAPTER 17

WHG stands for Walsall Housing Group. First time I heard about it from Gosia. It's one of the housing association in Walsall.

Because we had been living in such a bad condition after 4 years we decided to look for another place to live in.

John made the first move. One day he went to head office of WHG to ask how to apply for a house from them. They gave him website to go to, and told him what to do. Of course everything had to be done online.

We checked WHG website. It wasn't so complicated to apply. After we had fulfilled application online we were told what kind of documents they wanted to see. I sent required documents which we had gathered, and we could start to bid for WHG houses. I wanted some house close to where we were living. I like brick houses, not those with paint on them.

We had seen two properties altogether before we found the right one. One of them was in Bloxwich area. It was a flat above the shops. We didn't like it. Mess was all around it. The other house was very far from Walsall Town Centre. I hadn't even been there before. There was not even direct bus to Walsall. I didn't like the place, because it was more like a countryside. Too quiet for me. We wouldn't get it anyway, because somebody else had won that bid.

Third time we were lucky with John. We got to see the house we both liked, and it wasn't far from where we lived. The place is called Darlaston, and that's where we live up to this day.

We had to give up our old house. 'Good Childs' estate agent came to inspect the place when all our furniture was gone. She said she felt sorry for us to live in a bad property like that.

John gradually moved all our furniture, and clothes, and other belongings to Darlaston. We didn't even had to pay deposit to WHG. Rent in our circumstances back then was much smaller compering to the money we had paid to 'Good Childs'.

There are 3 bedrooms in our house, 2 toilets, kitchen, and a big garden. We have also fire place in the living-room.

We chose for our bedroom front room with John from the side of the street. Ewa decided to take the biggest bedroom from the garden side, and Pawel the smallest one on the same side. Kitchen is big. You go through the kitchen to the garden.

We had been waiting for this house around 6 months before we got it, but it was worth to wait.

I was extremely happy, and grateful to John to start this process of getting a council house for us. I felt like we'd won the lottery.

It made such a big difference to comfort of our life. Children were happy too.

We had to buy our own cooker, and put carpet in the whole house.

My parents helped us financially.

It's an exciting process to arrange new place to live.

Children were a little nervous. They didn't know what to expect. I told them not to worry. 'Some things will be better, and some worse in our new house'. There is not such thing as perfect place to live.

In my eyes our brick house isn't far from perfect.

We managed to buy, and connect our cooker. We also chose carpet with John, and had it fitted (brown with white dots). I bought curtains in the market in Walsall.

While we were slowly moving from old house to the new one my parents came to visit us. Thomas brought them by car. Maria was here too on that occasion.

Parents were the one to sleep in our new house first.

They like England. My father as a seaman had been to UK many times.

I don't know why they don't travel that much. Mother still works part-time. Father is helping her. They only go to Lodz where my father was born, and Szczecin which is close.

My mother likes the most going for short trips to Germany. Swinoujscie is situated on the border with Germany. They always go there together. They buy a lot of things in German supermarkets like cosmetics, or grocery products.

The nearest towns from Polish Swinoujscie are Ahlbeck, Herringsdorf, and Bansin.

Now when my parents have problem with walking they go everywhere by car.

I remember when I saw my mother for the first time with walking stick I was crying later on in bed. I felt so sorry for her. She had had an operation on her spine, but it didn't help her. She is walking with walking stick not to fall.

I think father is better in walking than mother. He had had a knee replacement surgery, and it helped him.

Mother loves to go out. She is so happy when she is out.

When we are there for summer holidays she always takes us to nice places in Swinoujscie, and to these nice German towns. She buys us clothes, shoes, ice-creams, waffels, and drinks.

Father every morning is going to do shopping, most of the time with Pawel.

Every day he buys fresh rolls, fruits, drinks, meat, eggs, sausages, you name it. We are not short of anything when we are there.

I love my parents. They are trying their best to make us happy while we are in their place. Usually we spent there 5 weeks during summer holidays.

We had a good time when parents were here. Before they had been planning to come here I was on the phone with them. My mother said' we are already packed, we have driver, we have money, and we are about to go'. That's how exited she was. She didn't sleep the whole night before the journey.

I think that deep down inside they love me, and my children. They just cannot say it.

With father I always have problems, because he is a joker. Whatever I say about our life he can turn it into a joke which I don't like. Sometimes I don't know if I should laugh, or cry. Mother is always laughing at his jokes. Sometimes we laugh together.

I miss my parents deeply. Children would like to visit them this summer too.

Pawel is in a process of getting his driving license. He will have his theory test tomorrow. John is teaching him how to drive. I hope he will pass. He said if he got his driving license he would go to Poland by car. Of course he wants his own car, but I don't think it's a good idea. Car insurance is expensive. He would be willing to go to part-time, or weekend work to maintain his car. Pawel is too talented to waste his talent. I definitely don't want him to go to work. John will let him to drive his car from time to time. Pawel has to learn, go to the University. He cannot end up like me with qualifications doing some random jobs. I want him to have a good job from the beginning.

The same I want for Ewa, but because of her illness she might struggle at work. Hopefully not.

John always says to our children that in this great country that they have endless possibilities when it comes to learning.

For example Emilia started nursery at the age of 2 free of charge part time. Now she is 5, and in reception. She loves going to school. I like her teacher very much. She is learning quickly. I'm so proud of her.

Everybody thinks their child is the best including me. I don't talk to another parents from Emilia's school so I wouldn't know.

To be honest after all these years living in Britain only just recently I have started to be more open in contacts with people in the streets, or neighbors. Most people who live on our street are elderly. These type of people I talk to the most. Younger people are too busy to notice me. Too busy working while 'I waste my time walking the street' like John would say.

I think I have just started to feel that I belong here. I've found my place on earth in our brick house.

I almost didn't work at all since we had moved in here.

I started to think seriously about having another baby. I had came of the pill, and I was waiting for it to happen.

In the meantime my brother with his wife came to live with us. They also wanted to make it in England. They didn't stay long in our place. As soon as Thomas had got a job they found their own place to live close to us.

My husband wasn't happy that they were here. He just doesn't like him. They have nothing in common with my brother.

Thomas is 5 years younger than me. We also have nothing in common. He is my only brother. Maria, his wife, is different than me(now they are after divorce). She is noisy, chatty, and very self-confident.

We didn't talk to each other too much while they were living in our house. They were sleeping in the living-room.

I was still suffering from depression (which I didn't know then). I was spending most of my free time in bed while Maria was downstairs. I was so ashamed of my lifestyle. Children didn't feel comfortable with them in our house too.

They were out a lot. John said that they liked to drink alcohol, and smoke.

Now they live in different places in Poland. Maria came back to her home town with their son. Thomas got married again, and has a new baby boy with his new wife.

Some people like adventures in their lives. Like them. People who never struggle, and have everything. They are bored of ordinary life, and cannot appreciate of what they have.

I'm trying to maintain what we have got which sometimes is hard. We are used to our comfort now, but it comes with a price. I don't want my children to feel worse than the others.

When you are used to something, and suddenly you lose it it's not a nice feeling at all. We know a lot about this rule. So many times we ended up without electricity, or wi-fi, car, or proper food.

John can make something out of nothing in the kitchen. But I don't. I like to have all ingredients to make a meal.

We have always done what we could, and we are still doing.

I like Darlaston. In the heart of this town there is supermarket called ASDA. We go there often, but most of grocery shopping we do in Lidl on weekly basis. There is Lidl in Walsall. Our Church is behind ASDA. We always walk there with children. I like going to Church. It's our obligation as Catholics to go to Church on Sundays. Faith, prayer is a good help how to live, what choices to make for me. I wish I could read Bible more often. It's always close to me on my table in the living-room. Sometimes I would like to push my children into God. But faith is so preciouses to me that I keep it deep down inside me not to lose it.

Everybody's way to God is different. I have been always close to God going to Church, and praying. It has been always helpful to me.

I cannot imagine to live in a countryside far from shops. I like towns better.

I grew up in a town, not very big one. I was studying at the University in big city called Szczecin. I liked it. I was even living there for a while after I had finished my education. Pawel was born there.

I was hiding my second pregnancy from parents, and the fact that I was still in contact with John who was in Jamaica.

It's so good to be independent. You can do what you like. I had been dependent on John for so many years that I hardly remember how independence feels like. I don't mean to be alone. I'm thinking about financial independence. It's good, but you must be careful not to go over your limit. You want to make yourself happy, your children, and your husband which is impossible. Always somebody will complain that they didn't get enough, and I feel sorry for myself, because I cannot please myself, and the rest of my family.

Besides everybody has different needs.

I don't buy a lot of things to the house. John always complains about that. I just don't like changes too much. Our house is perfect in my eyes. Some people change the design every season, but I simply cannot afford it.

The biggest problem when it comes to money to me is Ewa. She can say that there is nothing to eat in the house just after we've just done grocery shopping in Lidl. She is like a child who doesn't understand anything. Money she gets from College for 6 weeks she can spend in a week.

Ewa loves her food. We hardly ever eat take away. It's not healthy, and it's cheaper to cook at home. John doesn't like food like that, because he doesn't trust people who make it. He used to work in bakery in Jamaica, so he knows what workers do in food factories (sometimes very disgusting things). I don't really think about it. I just know it's good, because I don't have to cook it.

My husband is doing most of the cooking in our house. No matter if he is working, or not he is still doing that. I let him do it, because he is better cook than me.

Everything I cook I'd learnt from him.

Most of the time we have chicken on our menu. John says that soon we all will start to fly, because we eat so much chicken.

After those 7 years living in Darlaston we know many people around us. I have not made any friends since Gosia's times, but that's fine with me. It's enough to say 'hi' to people in the street for me, or smile.

John says the whole street knows us, because every time I go out with Emilia I shout telling her what to do, and what not to do. Most people drive here, and I always walk except when John takes us in his car. I try to be quiet, but she hardly ever listens to me so I lose it with her.

Before we moved in here we had been warned by our landlord WHG that some Asian people were complaining about racism in this area. We've never experienced any racism towards us so far.

There are many Asian people live among us. Most of them are hard-working people. I really admire their attitude towards work. Pawel has a lot of Asian friends at school. A lot of corner shops are run by Asians. Taxi drivers are Asians too most of all.

I don't know anything about their religion. I know about myself.

Everybody does what they can. That's what matters, and not the color of the skin.

We are one community. We respect one another paying attention to what we have in common, and not what is different.

We even used to have an Asian priest in our Church a few years ago.

Even Ewa's friend's family goes to our Church who is with Asian origin.

We all have to get on for our own good.

As I said before we had a good time when my parents were here. They bought a few little things to our new house like clocks to childrens' room, and special shelf for dvds. They like to buy in Argos. That's their favorite shop, Primark, Mark & Spencers, and Poundland.

I took them by bus to Walsall, and Wolverhampton. We had picnic in Arboretum park (Chinese take away).

It was very good to have them here. At least they know where we live. They don't have to imagine any more.

It's only a shame that they don't come that often. It's a shame that they don't live here permanently. I would like that very much so we could have more contacts with one another. I could help them with everything in our country.

Will it ever happen? I don't know.

My brother lives with parents with his new family. He might help them when they will need help. Whoever is far cannot help just like me.

Daughter is usually closer to mother than son. That's natural. That's why I think my parents should come to live in England pretty soon, before it's too late.

They have got each other, they are independent, but one day it will change. I don't want them to end up in a care home far from us. I would like them to be close to us so I could help.

Parents are proud, but deep down inside they know they will be in trouble one day.

Nothing is holding them back in Poland. They can sell the house they own, and help my brother to get a flat. The house is much too big for them. They used to rent rooms before, but they don't do that any more.

Of course it's up to them. It's not my decision. If they did that I wouldn't let them down, because I love, and miss my parents very much.

They had let me down, they had rejected me, but it's all forgiven.

John wouldn't be happy if they came to England to live. But I would be happy, because except from John, my children, and Gosia I have nobody here.

To be honest I don't even remember doing something good for my parents. I don't even send them cards for special occasion any more.

I live only for myself, my husband, and children from the longest time which is sad. I must be selfish. That's why parents don't want to talk to me on the phone, because it doesn't benefit them.

When I was working I bought for my father watch which he doesn't wear.

After all these years when I am an adult they could have got so many nice gifts from me. I could have taken them for holidays, and things like that.

I have nothing to offer them, and I have never had. Just to visit them once a year with children, and talk to them over the phone. That's it. They are used to it by now.

I hope parents are more satisfied with Thomas, my brother, since I'm such a failure.

It's a little more than a year when Ewa, and Pawel start new chapter in their life. They won't be under my wings any more.

I wish them good luck in adult life.

I tried my best for them to have a good childhood. Now their time to shine. I will be accompanied by Emilia. I won't be alone. It's good I have her. It's called 'empty nest's syndrome' when children leave family house, and parents are alone. I can imagine it must be difficult. You as a parent loses control over your children just like that. Some couples split up, because when children are gone there is nothing left between them any more. That's it. Job done. They go in different directions.

I would never want that to happen to us with John. I will do everything in my power to prevent it. I will hold on to him as much as I can, because we have to get old together.

John wanted to leave me so many times that I lost count. He doesn't like the way I act, and I will never change. He is not perfect either, because he has got a big mouth, and he can say everything to me. And John never says sorry. When we argue I hardly ever say a word. I'm waiting until he finishes his speech.

I never know where he is going. Sometimes he disappears for the whole day, and I don't know where he was. I don't know his friends, and if he has any.

One time he didn't come back home for a night. A long time he didn't pick up his phone. When he finally picked up he lied to me. He said he was somewhere with his cousin's husband Phill. He came back in the middle of next night. I was so mad with him. I told him that our house is not a hotel. Apparently he was in London visiting his friends.

Is it so hard to tell the truth? I hate this 'soon come' he always says while leaving the house.

I always like to go out with my husband by our car. It doesn't happen very often. At least once a week when we do grocery shopping in Lidl.

Most of places I go to are close to my house so I don't need to go by car. Only when I want to go to Walsall I need to take a bus, or by car.

I don't mind taking the bus. John is always rushing me when I'm doing my shopping which I don't like. I like to be slow.

I'm slow in anything. That's why I couldn't keep any of my jobs. I like to think a lot before doing something. My mother is slow like me. I got it from her genes, I guess.

But if it's a big shopping it's better to put it in the car, and come back home.

We have never been anywhere far in our new car which is a shame. Summer holidays are coming soon. I hope we will be able to do that.

It's good to leave your house from time to time. You can forget about problems you face there, and recharge your batteries.

I wish we could travel more often.

I miss sea side. I was brought up by the sea side. In West Midlands we don't have sea.

CHAPTER 18

We were trying for a baby with John for a few months in our new house. And after a year it happened. My period was late. I did pregnancy test, and it was positive. John after he had found out he kissed me.

I remember Ewa was that day on the school trip to one of those theme parks (Alton Towers, or Drayton Manor). I collected her from the bus, and on the way back home I told her about my pregnancy. She was excited. Later on at home I told Pawel my big news.

Soon after we had summer holidays. I went with children to visit my parents in Poland. We spent there a couple of weeks. I didn't have a courage to tell my parents about the fact that I was expecting. I was acting like a teenager while I was almost 40 years old.

At the end of our stay there I managed to tell them. They weren't happy for me. I wasn't surprised.

I came back home only to find out that my sister-in-law was pregnant too with her first child. So we were in this together.

Pregnancy was a happy time for me. I felt like on the cloud number nine. Everybody from my family was so overprotective towards me including John of course. My depression was gone.

I saw my midwife in a surgery regularly. I also had a couple of USG scans in the hospital.

We all wanted this baby to be a girl, and when the time came I was told on USG scan that it was going to be a girl. My due date was in March.

A few months before my due day I started to buy things for my baby. First of all we ordered a pram on Amazon. I was so happy when it arrived. Most clothes for her I bought in Asda.

I couldn't sleep thinking about all these cute little leggings, tiny socks, and body suites. We bought expensive jacket with pants in pink in Mother Care with John.

I also had to buy things for myself to take to hospital to give birth. I bought for myself two nighties, towel, dressing gown, and panties.

I couldn't believe in what was happening to me. Such a blessing.

I had delivery day set up, because I was going to have cesarean section again, just like with Ewa, and Pawel before.

When my older kids were born John was absent. I gave birth to them myself. With Emilia I had this support all the way through. That was one of the reasons why I wanted to have another child.

Just before my due date John chose a car online. The dealer was in Blackburn. We all went there to collect it. We liked the car so we bought it. It was good to own car again after almost 2 years without it.

My last appointment in a hospital a day before my operation with a midwife was such a disappointment, because she couldn't speak English (she was Italian). I was shocked that people like that can work in hospitals. It was my bad luck.

On the day of my delivery I called the hospital at 7 o'clock in the morning. They told me the time to come to the hospital later that day.

I was told to come at 12 pm. Children were at school. It was Wednesday. John took me to the hospital. Soon after I had arrived they started to prepare me for my op. I got change in hospital gown. I had to put on special stockings. John was all the time with me. I wasn't scared. It wasn't my first time so I knew what to expect.

First I got an injection in my back of anesthetics. After a couple of minutes when I didn't feel anything from my back down doctor started to operate on me. Not long after we heard cry of our little daughter. After she had been wrapped up in towel tight John took her in his arms, and he showed her to me. She was just perfect. Just after that he started to feed her. I couldn't breastfeed, because I was on my medications from bipolar disorder.

She was born around 3pm. That was the time when Ewa, and Pawel were finishing school. I looked at the clock in the operating table, and thought about them.

I'd chosen name before she was born. Emilia.

She had a little face, big eyes, and black hair.

They put me in a rest room after operation. John was taking care of our newborn baby while I was sleeping. After I had woken up I told him to go home, and bring Ewa, and Pawel to the hospital to meet her new sister for the first time.

It was very special, unforgettable moment when they all came. Ewa was a little disappointed, because Emilia was sleeping all the time.

First night I didn't take care of Emilia. Nurses were taking care of her. In the middle of the night I was told to have a shower by hospital staff.

In the morning my husband came, and brought me flowers, and teddy bear for Emilia. He also brought some food, and drinks. We had private room.

I spent in the hospital 2 nights only. Second night Emilia was crying. Nurse came to check on us. She said 'she just wants her mother'. So it was my time to comfort her.

On Friday I put on Emilia her pretty dress, and I was waiting impatiently for John to take us home. I got her red book, and my injections. I was told what would happen next by nurse.

John came with a car seat for Emilia. We went straight back home. I was so proud of us all. We did it!

We brought our newborn child home. The wait was over. There were 5 of us from now on.

Emilia was born a few days before Mother's Day. I remember on that day John with Pawel build my new pram. I loved it! The best present ever for Mother's Day.

Health visitor came to visit a few times. Everything was all right with Emilia. She was putting weight on. I had my stiches removed at home by midwife.

My plan was put in action. I had my third child. I couldn't be more happy than that. That was what I had needed. My family was completed.

Around Easter that year my parents came to visit, but they stayed in my brother's place. We spent a few days together. I could introduce Emilia to them.

It's good that they came, because later in the summer we couldn't go to visit them. Emilia didn't get her passport.

I applied for British passport for her, but it was a mistake. Later on she got Polish one.

Pawel in the same year joined football team. It had been his dream, and it happened. He had trainings once a week, and matches on Sundays. We were always going with him for the matches. Sometimes these pitches were quite far from home. He was happy doing that.

I was back on my regular medications for bipolar disorder. I couldn't wake up to Emilia to feed her at nights. Most of the time John was doing that.

Sometimes we both were awake at night. I remember these sleepless nights talking about our future.

By the age of 1 our talented child could talk, and walk. We were so proud of her. She was one healthy, and happy girl. We were lucky to have her. All we had to do was to treasure her.

Thomas, and Maria got a baby boy 2 months after Emilia. But next year, before Easter they all returned to Poland for good. My brother's wife was complaining about life in England after their son had been born. I even blamed myself for that. That I didn't pay her no mind when she was here. It wasn't a good decision, because a few months later they split up.

John was happy. My brother wasn't here any more.

Presence of my brother was a small problem to my husband. He had been on sick leave from the longest time for high blood pressure. Doctors couldn't control his high blood pressure, and he felt bad. He was only getting little money for sick leave. That was a problem to us. It was like that for a few months.

My parents were helping us as much as they could. Without their help it would be hard to survive. They always asked me if I had money, and the answer was always no. So they were sending again.

John always complains about the money. Even if he has it he is hiding from me. That's how he is trying to protect the little that he has for rainy days.

I never had any extra to go to the cinema, or swimming-pool. Only when we used to live with Mario we could afford it. Later on not any more.

For John it doesn't matter. Roof over our head, food on our table, and clothes on our back are important. Nothing else.

When Emilia had got her passport we could finally go to Poland for couple of weeks in the summer. I was so happy to present to my Polish family Emilia. New addition. My parents bought her a new pushchair – small one to fit in a car, and bus without a problem. Very nice one.

We had a good time there. Emilia was on the beach for the first time. She didn't like the water too much. She only liked to play in the sand. We were going to our favorite shopping center Corso to buy some clothes, shoes, cosmetics. We also were dining in different restaurants, and went for desserts to the café.

My mother was only free at the weekend. She was always organizing trips to Germany by car. There was not enough space in the car for all of us any more. Pawel sometimes was going by bike.

Every morning my father was going to do shopping with me, or Pawel for fresh rolls, something for dinners, drinks, and whatever we wanted while my mother was at work.

We always have a good time in my parents' place, but father sometimes exaggerates with his jokes. He is laughing at us in our face that we don't have money, and things like that.

We stay there too long. That's the problem. Later on they are tired of us.

Last time we were there two and a half years ago. It wasn't so good this time, because everybody was sick. We had to take antibiotics with Pawel for tonsilitis. John was there too for a few days. Emilia didn't want to eat anything there. That was a big problem. She is not used to polish meals. I also experienced side effects of my medicine a few times. When you are sick the best place to be is your home. But somehow we stayed to the end.

It's good for relationship to be apart for some time. You cannot be with your other half 24/7.

John always welcomes us back in a clean house. He always buys new things to the house while we are not there.

I love him to bits.

Later on we were preparing children to school, because September is round the corner. We arrive about a week before school starts. It's always good to be back home.

I remember a long time ago Pawel was crying after we had come back from Poland. But now he doesn't cry anymore. There is nothing to cry about. We live here, and my parents live in Poland. It's natural that we miss them. We don't see one another often. But once a year it's still better than nothing.

My parents basically don't know Emilia. She didn't grow up in their country. She cannot speak their language. They don't have any contact with her. They only know her from my stories. That's sad.

John told me not to teach Emilia any Polish, and I agreed. That was his decision, not mine. Now she doesn't understand when we talk with Ewa, or Pawel which makes her mad.

My youngest daughter doesn't listen to me which makes me mad. I keep repeating over, and over again the same commands, but nothing happens. Everything is 'no'. I hope it's just a phase, and she will grow out of it.

There are times when I don't know myself. It's like I'm lost. When you have children you have to be strong for them, but sometimes I'm weak. It's because I'm sick. There are good days, and bad ones.

During bad days you only wait for an evening to come to go to sleep to forget how bad you feel. When you wake up the feeling is still there. You don't have a courage to face the day. It's hard to do everything which ordinary people do without a problem.

It's a popular illness. Many famous people suffer from it like Mariah Carey, Catherine Zeta-Jones, or David Walliams, and Kerry Katona. That's not helping me. I am alone. I suffer alone. No one can take this burden from my shoulders.

Emilia started to walk, and talk very quickly. We have to run after her to protect her from danger. Only in her pram she was safe, but she didn't use it for a long time. She wanted to walk instead to explore. John let her go wherever she wanted despite the danger. The same in the shops. John let her be lost, and told me not to call her.

But until now she somehow survived, and nothing bad happened to her.

Now she is terrorizing everybody in the house to force her way. I cannot control her. She is hard to deal with.

I don't think Ewa, and Pawel were like that when they were at her age. Maybe I just don't remember, because it was a long time ago.

My life is pretty boring. I go to school with Emilia in the mornings. Later on I go to do some shopping. I cook dinner, and collect Emilia from school. We are waiting for Ewa, and Pawel to come back from school, and College.

I don't like to go out in the evenings. When I have to do that it feels strange. I feel like I belong to the house in the evenings. Sometimes (especially in the summer) evenings are long, and warm, but I am at home. I go to bed most times with Emilia. We talk a little bit, and later on we fall asleep. I don't know if it'll ever change.

My dream is to travel the whole UK. I can only make my dreams come true.

Everybody who is ashamed of me one day they will be proud of me. Everybody who doesn't believe in me will believe.

I believe in myself. That's what matters.

In England we don't have a lot of hot days in the summer.

When the weather is good there is always pressure to go out, and do something special. Now without a car (John has it) we cannot do much. We are bored of the nearest park. We would like to go, and explore new places.

Most of the days we just go with Ewa, and Emilia to the nearest supermarket. There is playground nearby too. That's our entertainment. Buy something sweet to eat, and drink, and go to that playground.

I don't want to complain, but our life could be more exciting. Just a little more.

Even when my husband was with us at home he hardly ever took us anywhere. He liked being at home. It was so disappointing. Most of the time he was driving on his own.

John likes space. He likes to be on his own sometimes. Nothing wrong with that. I think I always give him that space. I respect that need. Now he has too much of it.

I also have nobody to tell me what to do at home, and I like it. I do what I like, and when I like. It might sound terrible, but that's the way it is. There are as well positive sides of living apart. But of course most negative, and I want him back, because he is irreplaceable, and I love him. He was my first real love, and I want to stick to it.

This month is Ewa's nineteenth birthday. Last year she celebrated her birthday in a hospital. Hopefully she will be at home this year. As usual John won't even wish her happy birthday. They're always at war. Now it's even worse.

John cannot believe it how she turned her back at him. After all these years taking care of her. I don't know if they will ever talk again. I don't think so. She had never been under pressure from him.

We are close with Ewa now, but what if she ever turns against me? That would be unbearable. It might happen one day.

I cannot count on John any more. I won't be able to count on Ewa. Only Pawel, and Emilia will be left. Pawel pretty soon might leave the house, and go to University. It will be only me, and Emilia.

My future doesn't look rosy to me. I chose Ewa over John, and now I suffer consequences.

CHAPTER 19

Autism is a terrible illness. There is no cure for that, and it lasts until the end of your life. You struggle to make relationships with people, because you don't know how they feel. You don't like changes in your life. You prefer routine.

Autistic people are into something with passion, but very quickly they are board, and give it up.

They can be violent towards other people, and they can hurt them. They also can break things around them.

Ewa's autism is the reason why John is out of the house now.

When Ewa was 15 (the year Emilia was born) she started to act weird at the end of July. She came in the middle of the night to our bedroom, and said that daddy raped her. Somehow we managed to make an appointment with a gp the same day. She was seen by him alone. She told him the same story. Doctor asked if she wanted to press charges.

We came back home. She was still weird. In the evening we took her to Urgent Care Centre in Manor Hospital in Walsall. They decided for her to stay in the hospital overnight. Ewa was admitted to PAU pediatric unit for children. It was about 4 o'clock in the morning. I came by taxi home.

All those events were horrible to me. None of my children had never had serious illness like that before. I was in pieces.

I had a short sleep, and in the morning I prepared myself to go to the hospital to see how she was doing. John took me there with Emilia. He stopped from work.

Ewa didn't have a good night. She couldn't sleep the whole night. She was agitated walking in her room saying random things. There were two guards watching her the whole time in front of her room. She also didn't want to eat.I was told that she would be seen by child psychiatrist as soon as possible. We couldn't wait for that to happen, because with every hour she was deteriorating.

I stayed in the hospital with Ewa the whole day. I just went out for an hour to eat something. Ewa even refused her beloved McDonald's. Only music calmed her down. So we were there listening to music.

I understood her. I had been in similar position a few years before her illness.

The appointment with this psychiatrist was going to take place next day in the morning.

I left hospital around 9 pm. My daughter was in bed, but still she wasn't sleeping. John brought me back home.

Another morning in the hospital with Ewa was even worse. She hadn't been sleeping the whole night. She had been refusing food. We were waiting for that doctor. John decided to be there too.

It wasn't only psychiatrist there. There were also a few more people including social worker.

Ewa repeated the same story about being raped by her father.

I told them about my struggle with bipolar disorder, but it wasn't about me. It was about Ewa to get better.

Because me, and Ewa had similar problems with mental health problems doctor told us that it would be John to make any decisions.

Medicines were introduced to Ewa (the same as mine at that time), but smaller dose, and she was going to be transferred to different hospital. I made sure told them not to put her somewhere far from our house, because I don't drive.

But we didn't know when this transfer was going to be. The doctor was going to look for bed in a mental hospital for teenagers like Ewa.

John was a little mad. Ewa was refusing taking her medicines, and she wasn't getting better. We needed this bed immediately. There was no time to waste.

Fortunately doctor, and her team found a bed quite quickly for our Ewa. Nurse spread me that news. And it wasn't far from where we lived. In Birmingham.

Nurses knew that place. They said it was a nice, private hospital, but we didn't have to pay.

Ewa was in a bad state. She wasn't in a position to go nowhere. Special transport was organized for her to take her to that hospital in Birmingham.

Me, and a few nurses, and a guard were when we were leaving that ward.

It was about 7 pm.

Ewa was so scared. She didn't trust anybody on the way to that van. Of course she didn't want to go inside that van. Nobody could persuaded her to do that. At some point they wanted to put her back to the ward. In the same hospital, but I couldn't let this to happen. That would kill her for sure. Another day without sleeping, eating, and hallucinating. I stepped in. I asked them if I could go with her. Thankfully they agreed. Slowly she entered the van with me following her. She asked the driver for Capital radio station to turn it on. Van had bars to secure the driver. There were also two other women, NHS workers with us sitting at the back.

We didn't travel a long time. About 30 minutes on the motorway. I was trying to figure out where it was, but I didn't know this part of Birmingham.

I had £10 in my pocket.

Just as we entered the Priory Hospital in Edgbaston there was different approach to Ewa. They welcomed her with hot chocolate.

We talked to the psychiatrist there, and I was told to leave. I could come back anytime to visit my daughter.

When I was free it was 11 pm. I was so scared being far from home. To make the matters worse there was no network connection on my mobile to call my brother to come to pick me up. John didn't know where I was.

I looked around, and started to walk towards the main street. I noticed a bus stop. I decided to check what buses come there.

There was bus to Wolverhampton. That was hopeful. Although it was late this bus was still running. I jumped on this bus. It was a long route. My mobile still didn't work. I couldn't call John to tell him where I was.

In Wolverhampton I missed the last bus to our place. I had to take a taxi. John paid taxi fare.

I told him all about my adventure. One good thing about that was that I knew exactly where Ewa was, and how to get there by public transport.

It was good to be home, because I don't like to be far from home when it's late. I'm not scared of people, or that something bad can happen to me. I just have this strange feeling that I belong to my house in the evenings.

I'm active in the mornings, and lunch time, but afternoons, and evenings I spend almost always at home.

When I'm done with dinner I like to watch Poitntless, BBC News at 6, The One Show, and Eastenders.

Of course most of the time I don't watch anything, because somebody else is watching something else from my family.

Pawel loves to watch sport on TV: football, basketball, hockey, and American football.

Emilia watches all kind of stuff on You Tube. Only Ewa doesn't watch too much on television.

John likes news, and cowboy movies.

My time to watch is in the morning: Good Morning Britain, This Morning, and Loose Women.

Of course I don't watch those either, because of house work: cooking, cleaning, or washing.

I used to watch more on television when I was younger with John.

Even a few years ago we were with children fans of X-factor, and The Voice. We also watched Miranda- a comedy series.

I like when we are all together with children in a living-room. But sometimes they are in their rooms.

On Sundays I watch Songs of Praise, and Countryfile.

We have one television in the house at the moment from the longest times.

We don't like when Emilia is watching You Tube on her phone, or on television. But all of us do something on our phones for a long period of time so she wants to be like us. But she isn't. She is only little girl, who believes in almost everything she sees.

Ewa is making vlogs from the longest time. She has her channel on You Tube. I think she started about 6 years ago. She can really chat, and is very funny. I am very proud of her.

I am an old-dated person. I don't like to use something new. But now it's required. Every move you make you have to pick up your phone, or laptop first. Smart phone I mean. Hand-written letters, and ordinary phones are going to disappear soon for ever. That's what I'm used to as an old-fashioned woman.

It will never go away. I have to accept it as it is.

Sometimes it's just you, and your laptop, or smartphone, and you cannot do something, and there is no help from anywhere. That terrible. You know you have to do that, but you don't know how.

IT specialists wanted to make our life easier, but instead of that for some people like me, and John.

I'm doing this things for us. And there is always something to do. John only is looking for documents all the time.

Even in the street it's shameful to ask somebody for direction since we have Google Maps on our phones, and sat-nav in our cars.

It's good that they still print magazines, and books, and there is normal television.

The worst is that you just have to have wi-fi at home which is expensive to have. You can also have data on your phone which costs too.

Homework is online for children.

To make things running you need to have electricity which comes at a cost too.

It's a never-ending circle of expenses which put pressure on people like us.

If you don't pay, for example, wi-fi the company providing it will disconnect it.

Now there is a lot said in media about protecting the environment. Everybody has different opinion. Poor people different, and rich ones different. Those two categories have various point of view. If you are struggling, or had been in the past you know how it feels like. Rich people have never been through it what you has been. That's why those two groups don't understand each other.

How to protect the environment when you cannot feed your children? You can recycle, you can avoid littering, but what else you can do?

I remember we went to London for 2 days last summer. Afterwards charges came (congestion charge, and emissions zones). It wasn't little money, but we had to pay it.

Before we had our old car with 2004 plates. We wanted to park somewhere, but the prices in the center were horrendous. And the older car the more you pay. It wasn't small money either.

We can save electricity, gas, and water to protect the environment, and teach that to our children. That's all we can do as poor people. Nothing else.

My father once said to me that poor people only complain on television while rich ones are quiet making money. There must be something in it.

I don't know if I am rich, or poor. All I know is that I have children who love me, and, because of that, I feel the richest person in the world. I'm doing my best to bring them up.

John always tells me that we were poor, but I don't think so any more.

Ewa's new hospital in Birmingham was very nice. Straight away she started to take her medications which was very good. I was very happy about it, and relieved. She had there her own room with a bathroom.

At the beginning someone was always by her door, even at night to make sure she was all right. She started sleep, and eat well.

We tried to visit her 3 times a week. She could call us from the hospital phone whenever she wanted to.

There were boys, and girls at her age, or older. No adults.

She was on the same medications as me, but smaller dose. Now I take completely different ones.

We could visit Ewa whenever we wanted. Emilia was 5 months then. Pawel was 13. We all going to visit her by car.

We didn't know how long she would be there.

Ewa of course demanded a lot of snacks, fruits, and drinks. We also were buying her clothes

John always says to save money, and things for rainy days, but we hadn't done that. When it's an emergency like that we have nothing. Ewa didn't even had dressing-gown, and slippers.

Thankfully my parents stepped in. They send money every week to support us. Once even they sent £300 when our car was broken, and we had to fix it. I don't know what would we do without them?

After around 10 days Ewa wasn't on 1 to 1 any more. They let her leave the room.

She wasn't complaining. I knew she would stay there a long time. There was no doubts in it. The most important that she wasn't that far from home.

I knew that because when I was 19 years old I had been in similar hospital for 3 months, before they discharged me.

Ewa enjoyed our visits. I also liked to visit her.

She got sick in July. In September she was supposed to come back to school, but she didn't, because she was still in the hospital.

After a few weeks in the hospital she started slowly come out of it with her health care assistant for short walks to the nearest shop, which was Tesco Express. She even once went to Costa Café for hot chocolate. Later on they allowed us to take her out for an hour, or more by car.

The nearest supermarket from Ewa's hospital was Morrisons with Café inside. To get there it took us 5 minutes by car.

At first we were taking her to Morrisons, because she was getting short time out. But later on Ewa was getting a few hours, so we were going to Birmingham City Centre. We were doing shopping, eating in McDonald's, or our favorite Buffet.

In September she had a kind of lessons in the hospital. Later on they were taking her to school by car just to see how she was doing.

At the end she was even allowed to come home for a weekend. Baby steps.

In October we went to London with John, Pawel, and Emilia to get visa for John to go to Switzerland. He got his visa the next day. He already had his ticket booked from London Stanstead to Geneva. He took a train to London, and later on a plane to Switzerland. Members of his family collected him from the airport

His sister with her family had recently moved into a big house in Vallorbe. She is very rich. They travel a lot with her husband, and eat in fancy restaurants all over the world.

I don't know how people can travel so much. Where do they take money for that.

The same is my cousin Ewa. She travels a lot too, but at least she doesn't go abroad so often.

I wasn't very worried about John leaving for Switzerland. He deserved the break.

Besides my parents were going to come to visit us during this time John was going to be away. I had something to look forward to.

He had a good time in his sister Margaret's place. His mother from America was also there. They all even went for a trip to France by boat. I was happy for him. He doesn't see his mother often.

My mother, and father came to visit us for a few days when Ewa was still in the hospital in October. They came especially to see how Ewa was doing. My brother collected them from the airport in London.

Thomas then had his first baby too so he was busy. Of course he was working, and his wife was at home with baby boy called Leon, who was born 2 months after our Emilia.

He took us once, or twice to Ewa's hospital to visit her, and brought us back.

One time all of us including Emilia in her pram visited Ewa travelling by bus.

My parents were already walking with walking sticks. I felt so sorry for them that they had to make that journey on the bus. Even I was exhausted afterwards. I felt like we went to the end of the world, and back. It was getting cold. Days were short.

While John was still in Switzerland doctor was about to discharge Ewa. She was waiting for John to come back home.

In the meantime my parents went back home. That left me a lot of money. I bought for that money X-Box One for Pawel. He was so happy.

We had a meeting in the hospital just after John had came back home from his vacation.

They were a few people representing different sectors. Psychiatrist of course, social worker, and even one woman from Ewa's school. And me, John, and Emilia.

We were told the diagnosis. Autism. We were shocked with my husband. We thought autism was condition for little children, not for 14 years old girls.

Ewa was ready to be discharged. It was a happy moment when we were taking her home for good. Very happy.

She went back to school, and was doing well. Slowly she was back to her normal-self.

We knew that she would always be autistic, and we might have similar problems like that in a future.

CHAPTER 20

When you are a foreigner in a strange country after a while you need to apply for a special permit. There are different requirements for different nationalities.

John comes from Jamaica. He managed to get a visa to come to the UK, because he is my husband, and I am EEA national.

I had had to get a job in UK first to sent documents to John who from the longest time had been in Jamaica.

I did it quickly. I had got a job, and I could get papers for my husband.

He got his visa before Christmas 2005. He was ready to leave Jamaica for UK.

They gave him 6 months visa in Embassy in Kingston.

When your visa is up and you want to stay longer you need to apply for a permit in Home Office.

John had applied for 5 years permit through the solicitor. The whole process had been long. We had had to give so many documents including our passports, our Polish ids, children's birth certificates, our pay slips, bank statements, and many more.

John's solicitor got permit for him for 5 years at the end. We were so happy.

Time passes quickly, and after these 5 years he needed another permit. This time he had a chance to get a permanent one.

But he had started to apply too late, and as a result of that he lost his job.

We were in shock when it happened. He had been working there a couple of years. He got 2 weeks notice only.

It was a good job. He had a contract. After this one he wasn't going to find another one good like that.

We went to the same solicitor's office to start the process of applying for permanent permit this time for John. We had gathered all the documents, and we were waiting for an outcome.

After a while John got his decision from Home Office. And the decision was 'no'. He was turned down.

Another shock. Not only he had lost his job, but also he didn't get his permit. That was too much to bear.

We could go to court to challenge this decision. It wasn't very expensive to go to court so we decided to do that.

We had paid the fee, and we were waiting for a hearing. We were going to be represented by solicitor, but different one.

The reason we hadn't got it in the first place was down to me. I should have been John's sponsor in UK. What kind of sponsor was I without a job, or any benefits for sick people?

That's why we lost our appeal in court.

We had came back to our solicitor again to ask her what to do, what our options were (if there were any). We were told by her that John should apply again for 5 years permit. That was our only choice.

So we had gone for it, and John quite quickly got his permit for 5 years again.

That was the end with problems with permit.

So many people are dreaming to live in UK. They would do everything to get here. In illegal boats through English Channel, underneath lorries. One African man even came to UK underneath a plane. Of course he didn't make it. His body fell down in somebody's garden in Richmond. A few months ago 34 people died in a lorry from some Asian country. They apparently froze to death inside this truck.

UK takes a lot of refugees. That's good.

It's a difficult decision to make for the government. Should they stay, or rather leave our country?

Some people in England don't want them here. They think they would be worse off because of them.

Refugees are like us, and they need what we need. Food, clothes, cosmetics, somewhere to live, and many more things. Maybe they are not used to luxury which we have. Maybe their houses look different in their countries, or they are damaged by war.

But they deserve a chance.

To be afraid of refugees is racism.

Women in Britain are fighting for their rights not to be made to wear high heels by their bosses to work. One of them said 'what are we talking about?', and she showed a few centimeters of high heel.

It's the same with color of the skin. What are we talking about?

Some black, Chinese, or Asian people are sensitive when it comes to color of their skin. They think, for example, that they cannot get a job, because of that.

I just like black men. I cannot help myself. When I start to see them in England coming back from vacation in Poland my heart is pounding.

Pawel is a handsome, young man, Ewa is pretty, and Emilia too.

I want them to be proud of who they are just like John is. I hope that their dreams will come true.

With dreams it's like with an illness. You suffer, you want to get better. After some time you recover, and you don't see the difference.

Every day is similar to one another, but sometimes there are surprises. You carry on with your duties. There are better days, and worse. But from time to time you know life is worth living. You just stop, and think how much you have achieved throughout these years. It might be to look at your children's life, at work, at friends, or wherever. This is me on this earth, I matter, and I am amazing. Sometimes it's difficult to believe it, but it's true.

I simply love my life. It's a gift from God, and I must cherish it.

CHAPTER 21

When John was trying to get this permit he couldn't work. We were relying on Tax Credit, Child Benefits, and some money sent from my parents. Housing Benefits were paying our rent.

It lasted a long time (more than a year). From hand to mouth. That's the life we lived. Thanks to my parents we weren't hungry.

At the end of year 2017 I managed to get a job in a warehouse in Lidl for 2 weeks only. John had to take me there, and brought me back, because bus connection was bad. I would have to take 2 buses, and walk a little bit. I was doing afternoon shifts. My duties were to scan non-food products, and put them on the belt, or pallet. When the pallet was full I had to drug the whole pallet to different place. These things were, for example, sewing machines, tools, furniture, clothes, shoes, books, toys. So some of them were very heavy. Despite that many women worked there.

I was one of them. Again in a hard job, not for me.

I lasted there 2 weeks. We had been told by work agency that it was going to be job only for 2 weeks. I was disappointed, but quickly agency found me another job in a company called Wiggle, a few minutes walk from my house.

Hope was back. There were long, 12 hours shifts. I was going to be rich.

Wiggle was a warehouse with sport equipment. My duties were to scan products, pack them into boxes, and stick the label with address on them.

They had these targets. Every morning we had those meetings to motivate us to reach their targets. The time was before Christmas.

Many people were working for them. This warehouse was huge. I had never seen anything like that before.

That scared me. Even to use the toilet you needed to scan special card.

I don't know how long I was there for. It couldn't be a long time. These 12 hours shifts were killing me.

One day when I was at work I felt bad. I couldn't continue my shift. I just left not to tell anyone. I would not even know who to tell. Everyone acted like a boss.

I was back there once more, but bad feeling made me go home again.

That was the end of my work in Wiggle. I didn't succeed again. Why everything went always wrong with my employment?

Afterwards I was in bed, and didn't feel like doing nothing. I had spent my salary, and we were broke again.

Nobody from my family were mad with me. They felt sorry for me. I was in a low mood again. I like to be exited, but I don't like to feel down. What excites me is money.

New Year started 2018. John still hadn't got his permit. I had to go to work no matter what. I started to look for one again.

I didn't look for it a long time.

One Polish woman from work agency in London found me a job as a pharmacy assistant band 2 in hospital pharmacy in Birmingham. It was quite far from where we lived. John had to take me in the mornings to the tram stop by car. Tram was taking me to the center of Birmingham. From there I had to take a bus to this hospital. It took me about one, and a half hours to get to work.

I started the 5 of February 2018.

I was so proud to get a job like that. Nearly according to my qualifications (I am pharmacy technician, not assistant).

I was working in distribution section of the pharmacy. My duties were: packing medicines into red boxes for different wards of the hospital. I had a list, and I was working as stated in that list. I was taking orders for medicines from another hospitals over the phone. I was checking expiry dates of medicines on our shelves.

There were 3 of us in distribution: Adam, Tanya, and me. Tanya was the one who taught me everything about the job. She had been employed there 3 months before me. She didn't have qualification in pharmacy at all.

Medicines are similar everywhere in the world. I know a lot about them. I was a good student in Poland, and I have learnt a lot.

Adam didn't have any pharmacy qualifications either.

In Poland people without special diplomas cannot work in pharmacies. The only person without it is a cleaner.

So how people less qualified than me can teach me how to do the job?

It's really strange that I let something like that happen to me.

I respect all people, but there is space for anybody somewhere.

Adam had been a porter in that hospital before.

I shouldn't have taken this job, but I didn't have a choice.

In Poland I could concentrate on medicines, and customers. To dispense drugs, and give advices to people over the counter. We did everything on the computers.

I loved my jobs in Poland. John was so proud of me serving customers in a white uniform.

I like to help people, and pharmacy jobs are all about that. I didn't lose my talents in Poland, unlike here. Instead of helping people I was doing all kinds of things far from that without any satisfaction.

I started work in my mother's shop with herbs, and medicines. We started together. Now it's 22nd year she is running it. She is the best.

I am the best too in my field. I might not work for a long time now, but I still remember my knowledge, and experience I had gained in those a few years in Poland. My mother still believes in, and is proud of me. She said to children one day 'your mother isn't a cook, or cleaner, she is pharmacist'. She knows me from the beginning of my life, and knows what I am capable of.

I had always been a good student starting in primary school, high school, and in my Medical College.

No one acknowledges it in England.

Maybe it's my fault. I was always picking up the simplest jobs to get just to prove a point.

My husband was always telling me throughout these years that I was better than that, and I should have done better. He always says 'if I only had a half of qualifications you have my life would be better'. But I had never listened.

Registration with General Pharmaceutical Council costs £500 plus translation of Polish documents. I've never done it. If it was done, I would be able to work as a pharmacy technician in UK.

It's a responsible work to deal with drugs. You cannot get distracted not to make a mistake. People want to get the right medicines. One mistake can cost somebody's life.

I was always trying to be careful, and accurate.

Every boss in Poland was happy with my work, and I had never had any problems.

It's just different system here than in Poland. There are many labels to put on medicines, and bags. They don't have it in Poland. They assume that customer is directed by the doctor how to take medicines.

Here a lot of people get medicines for free. Isn't that amazing? In Poland you always have to pay something.

NHS is good.

The things which I hated the most in my new job was answering the calls. You never knew what they would want from you. The worse when they were calling from the wards. I never knew where were their boxes, and where they would be delivered. When Adam, and Tanya were topping up the wards (it means to take orders for medicines), or they were on their breaks I always was so scared. I was just hoping, and praying that our phone won't ring. But it rang. Not always I was in troubles. Sometimes not.

This job in hospital in Birmingham was going to be my dream job, but it wasn't. It ended bad, and quickly.

My side effects of my medicine for bipolar disorder were getting from bad to worse. Approximately once a week I had to leave work earlier, because I felt bad.

First couple of times I was telling my manager that I had a headache. She let me go home earlier. But eventually I had to tell her about my illness.

Every time I felt bad my way back home from work was terrible. I couldn't see. My eyes were going up. When I was changing in Birmingham City Centre bus to tram I was just praying to God for car, of bus not to kill me. From the tram stop John usually was picking me up. I had had to call him before to tell him that I would be earlier, which wasn't easy either. As soon as I had reached our car, I knew I was safe. At home I was going straight to bed waiting until I would feel better.

Of course I wasn't paid for these hours at work that I had lost.

In June I was dismissed, but in August they called me to bring me back to work. I lasted until November. That was the end of not such a dream job after all. It was a few weeks before Christmas.

I was devastated again. John told me it was unfair dismissal so I wrote a letter to my manager in hospital that I would like to complain about losing my job just like that. My agent from this work agency called me. She told me to apologize for writing this letter to my manager. I was surprised. She was trying to frighten me that if I didn't do that I would never get another job in these hospitals (three of them were somehow connected). Of course I didn't allow her to frighten me. I didn't apologize.

Thankfully in the meantime John had got his permit, and could work again.

My husband is not so young any more. With every year of our life it's harder, and harder to get settled in a new job. He had been getting jobs through work agencies, and was losing them after a few months. Nigh shifts, afternoon shifts, you name it.

He likes to keep busy, but in his last job he didn't even last 2 days.

I had been trying to persuade him to change his career. To do some course to become somebody else, but he didn't like to do that. Maybe one day he will listen to me. I hope so.

His optician told him that he could be a guard. There are many courses available. If he only wanted it he would be proud of himself.

I'm proud of him. I had always wanted to have a hard-working man in my life. And I got one.

17th of July it will be 20th anniversary of our meeting with John which we never celebrate. In John's opinion there is nothing to celebrate. Day like every other day.

I wish we could take children to Switzerland, and show them when we met with daddy.

I cannot believe we've known each other so long. So much we've been through. Separation, persecution, poverty, and homelessness.

It's so easy to reach the bottom of existence.

But with God in your heart you know it's only temporary. You just have to wait for better times.

I hope my children won't have to go through times like us. We had been suffering. I don't want them to never ever suffer.

They have to be somebody in this country, and feel good.

I think they are going in the right direction. Pawel has John to look up to, and Ewa, and Emilia have me.

We are good parents. That's why they keep close to our house. They feel well here. We should be proud with John, because of that.

At the beginning when you have your first child you don't realize that this road with him, or she is never-ending. You buy this little bath, crib, cute blankets, and clothes, and you think 'that's enough'. But it's not. That's just the beginning of being a parent. It's never-ending journey of joy, pleasure, responsibility, and worry.

Nothing cannot compere to seeing smile on your child's face. But there are also tears, and tantrums.

It's a challenge to bring up children.

My oldest daughter Ewa doesn't live with us any more. She had another break down a week ago. She was taken by ambulance in the middle of the night to A&E. She had been violent towards me. I was scared of our safety.

She is now in special accommodation in Walsall Town Center. There are support workers in an office next to her flat. I cannot take care of her any more.

I was so mad with her, that I even couldn't look at her. It had been happening before many times, but never that bad like this time.

No John, no Ewa. There are only three of us in the house: me, Pawel, and Emilia.

Last time we were in Poland my brother was avoiding me after what he had done (he had cheated on his wife).

Long months I couldn't forgive him. But now I see he is a good father. Very often he brings his son from previous relationship Leon to Swinoujscie which is good. My parents are helping him to take care of their grandson. He also has one more child called Julek with his new wife, who is 4 months now.

When people split up, there is fault on both sides.

You cannot take things for granted.

Just like me, and John. We live separately. Most of the days I'm alone, expect weekends when he comes. I have to make my own decision, and face challenges like every other single mother.

You cannot judge people, because everyone has different story, which you don't know. You only know your story.

I used to feel sorry for my brother's first wife, but not any more. In the summer she went to the mountains for holidays without his son. Thomas had to take care of him while she was there.

I judge again. I did everything with my children. Maria likes to send her son to Thomas's place too often.

Children always suffer when parents split up. Thomas now have more responsibilities. It's good that parents help him.

I don't know how I could have been so clever to stick to John all these years. Somehow I always knew that children needed both: mother, and father.

Just like Holly Family. St.Mary, St.Joseph, and Jesus. Joseph is taking care of Mary, and Mary is taking care of Jesus.

My parents didn't split up either.

You just have to give a 100% every day to have a happy marriage, or relationship. I know that's a lot, but you have to put that effort. Every little detail matters.

There are many benefits of being together. You have somebody to count on.

In case of emergency your partner is by your side supporting you.

If you have children your partner can help you to take care of them.

Every couple complements each other. Everybody is good at something, and that's what each of us put into relationship.

We are like two pieces of heart with John, which matching each other. If one part is lost there is no possibility to replace it. We would never find a missing piece.

I am serious about that. I hope John feels the same way too.

He has moved out, but he keeps coming back, and answers my calls. He still sees children, and help them as much as he can.

We still make love. He still tells me that he loves me.

Our life is not simple. We have got as many complications as we possibly can.

It's probably, because we had started to see each other so quickly, and there was nobody to give us any good advice.

The first good advice I got from Patricia (John cousin). She had told me to get contraceptive pills, before John was going to came to England from Jamaica. It meant a lot to me. It was very thoughtful of her.

She had seen me struggling with my two little babies before. I'm very grateful to her for that.

John says that when he is inside me he feels like in heaven. Sex is very important to him. Without it he would be unhappy.

I like everything he does to me in bed.

He was my first lover, and hopefully the last one. I cannot imagine to be with somebody else.

His beautiful black skin turns me on.

CHAPTER 22

Our house where we live now is a Council house.

A few months ago I got for the first time money from JobCenter for my illness. I was so happy about that.

How many hours I spent in the Council, and CAB to search for financial help. Too many. Sometimes we were going there with John. Very clever people work in CAB. They are volunteers. Whatever the problem, they can solve it. They only don't deal with immigration matters.

Especially helpful to me was Julie. She has big knowledge. I really admired her. She walks with two walking sticks, and still comes to the office to help people like us.

John's favorite adviser was Dave. One time he even gave some money to John.

Britain is a country where you feel safe. Nothing bad can happen to you. Free advice, free medicines for those on law income, free NHS service, and dentist.

I don't know how it is to live in other countries, but I know that to live in UK is good.

Now when I am on my own I rely on benefits only. They pay me good money. If only I could manage to that money we would have enough.

Pawel is helping me to manage money which is good. He is good at saving money.

I thought he didn't like that responsibility, but I was wrong. He can handle it. He is now man in the house. In November he would be 18 years old.

How much I would like to give a lot back to this country.

So far I have only been taking from workers. I have been using other people's service.

I would like to be useful too.

I remember when I was going to that work in hospital in Birmingham I felt good. I knew I was doing something important.

Since then I hadn't been doing nothing for other people. Even in the Bible is said' who doesn't work shouldn't eat'.

My father had been working all his life, and he didn't receive any benefits.

Sometimes people abuse the system. They can work, but they stay on benefits,

The best is Universal Credit. We got it in 2019. John had lost his job in October the same year, and then we applied for UC. We had to wait 6 weeks for the decision. We had nice Christmas this year. We could buy nice presents for everybody thanks to UC.

I know that all these money comes from taxes to help people like us.

Even John sometimes had been complaining about that. He was working, paying taxes just to support some unfortunate people. Now he is an unfortunate one.

Situation can change just like that(quickly). People on the top can fall on the bottom.

That's why you have to respect work, and save money, because your future is unknown.

My example proves that. A little more than 2 months ago I had my whole family at home. First John had moved out, and later on Ewa was gone from the house.

What can I do about that?

Life surprises us from time to time. People make inversible decisions which change everything.

I first had chosen Ewa over John, and told him to move out, because they didn't get on well with her. Now Ewa is also gone, because of her illness. She is on her own now living in support accommodation in Walsall Town Centre.

John doesn't want to come back to my house, because he doesn't trust me any more.

My situation is more, and more complicated. I cannot believe in what is happening to me. It looks like we will never be one, big, happy family again.

What have I achieved in life so far?

I always thought that children were my biggest achievement, and my marriage to John. From material things this house, and our new car.

Is that enough?

I don't know. I'm fulfilled. It's enough for me.

What else could I possibly want?

Now I have to thank God for every day of my life, because it hadn't been always like that before.

We've come to the point that we have everything we need for our comfort.

I don't know if the rest of my family thinks the same as me. Kids probably not. They always want something new. So far only Pawel cares about money, and how much things cost.

It has taken us long years to get where we are now. It didn't just happen overnight.

That's why I respect John, and his work. It's mostly down to him why we are so happy now.

One time he had to take 3 buses to get to work when he couldn't drive. He used to work night shifts, afternoon shifts, and mornings.

Only John knows how hard he worked to put bread on our table, and keep roof over our heads.

Most people work until they are retired. That's how life is organized.

John always says that I'm used to 'free mentality', because I come from Poland which had been communist country before.

It's nice to get something for free.

When I'm alone in town I don't need to spend money on drinks, or food. But when I am with children it's a different story. They are thirsty, hungry e.t.c.

John isn't impressed by any restaurant. He only buys KFC from time to time.

Anyway. We don't have enough money for take aways. Ewa would order all the time, but it cannot happen. We only can afford ingredients in a shop to cook at home. That's the cheapest way.

I don't like cooking too much. But we have to eat. I don't learn new recipes. I'm afraid to waste money on new ingredients, and that I won't succeed.

I like cakes, but I don't bake too much. I know two recipes for cake, and I repeat them over, and over again.

When women talk about cooking around me I just don't say anything, because I have nothing to say. I am not interested in that.

I prefer other topics like gossip about other people.

When you stay alone all problems are on your head, and only you can solve them. The worst is that you cannot share your worries with anybody.

Children have to stay out of it. They have their own problems.

The worse is when you get sick. There is nobody to take care of you, and help you with the children.

For somebody like me, who doesn't have any friends, it would be the end of the world.

I know I've lost my chance with John, but at least he comes from time to time, and I can call him. It means a lot to me.

When he comes it's like a holiday. I am always counting down the nights to these special days.

It's my fault, and now I'm living in a kind of fantasy world. I don't know what future will bring for us. He says he loves me, but the longer you live on alone the more you get used to it. I don't want us to get used to it, because it can be dangerous for our relationship.

Anything can happen with death included, and children are left behind.

A long time I haven't been in Church. I love Church. I pray at home, but it's not the same. To see all those people is so good. I'm not alone who loves God, and wants to obey his rules.

Last time I was there a few weeks ago Emilia got lost. I just went to the toilet, and told her to wait outside the Church. But she didn't. I left the toilet, and she was nowhere to be seen. I quickly started to think where she could have been. She wouldn't come back to church. I started to call her name. People were leaving Church. I decided to go on the road. And there she was. My friend from Church Beatrice had stopped her. Emilia was on the way back home.

I was so grateful to Beatrice for stopping her. I would have lost her. That's the thing I'm afraid the most.

It's been years since I'm making those excuses not to go to Church. It's hard to wake up, the weather is bad e.t.c. Time to put stoppage to it right now. It cannot continue like that right now. When I finally go to Church I'm very happy.

In Poland I was going to Church more often. There are more Church services on Sundays there than only one like here.

And one more thing. I can never confess my sins here. I only do that when I am in Poland, because you only can do that before Mass which is very early (Mass starts in our Church at 8:30 am).

I like to confess my sins. It's like to get another chance from God to be good.

I have always been close to Church in Poland. Faith helps me throughout my life.

When I was struggling alone with Ewa, and Pawel long months without John God was with me. Step by step. Night by night. You can do it alone where there is nobody to help you. Besides you have no choice. At the end of the day you can be proud of yourself. Yes, I did it!

I have this character that I don't like to ask anybody for help. I'm shy. Good that I can do a lot of things on my own.

My illness doesn't stop me from doing every day duties. I am happy about that.

I'm also glad that Ewa is quite independent. Maybe she is autistic, but most of the time she knows what she is doing.

The most important for everybody to have a routine. That's how you know what to do.

For example my routine is like that: I take Emilia to school. I pray on my Rosary. I eat breakfast. I check my phone. Then I'm trying to write. After dinner, when children are back from school, I take it easy. I relax. In the evening I put Emilia to bed. I might do a little more writing after she falls asleep.

Ewa always asks me what she should do. Even now when she is on her own.

Emilia continually knows what to do. If it's not phone it's YouTube on television. She might play with blocks, or other toys. She is very creative. She enjoys doing crafts.

Not to mention Pawel. He has a lot to do. If he is not watching sport on television he is doing his training in the garden (running up, an down the stairs), riding his bike, playing on X-Box, or doing something on his phone (don't ask me what).

John's routine, if he is not working, is staying in bed the whole days.

Every day you have to repeat the same things over, and over again. Weekends might be a little different. I don't complain. I love my life.

I'm good at making plans for myself, and for my family. But not everybody agrees with my plans.

John doesn't like to be told what to do. He likes his own ideas.

Men shouldn't listen to women. Otherwise they would end up bad. It had been very difficult to persuade him to do something. Now, when he doesn't live with us any more it's easier. He is trying to be nice to everybody.

If Thomas didn't listen his wife Maria maybe they would still be together. She insisted on leaving Great Britain for

Poland. He didn't want to do that, because he was satisfied with his job. He even was going to do some course for free connected with delivering goods.

It's his life, and he makes his choices.

We are not those young kids with my brother any more. We are big people.

Childhood is long gone. I am older. I should find the way to approach him.

I wrote this story of my life to worn people that falling in love with a person from different country, and with different complexion of the skin can be challenging.

To be a foreigner in a strange country is hard at first, but it's worth to stay in a country like Great Britain. When the time passes you know more, and more about how this country operates.

You don't have to be scared. Just be yourself, and people will accept you. Nobody is perfect.

I'm really thankful for Great Britain to welcome us like that. The list of positive things about this country is long, and I could go on, and on, and on...I'm not going to do that.

So many people had been involved in enabling us to come here who I thanked at the beginning of my book.

Now I know. I love this country, and I cannot imagine to live somewhere else.

THE END

Lightning Source UK Ltd.
Milton Keynes UK
UKHW012153060122
396733UK00001B/55